Exploring the Treasures of Vatican II

Exploring the Treasures of Vatican II

James H. Kroeger

**Claretian
Publications**

**Jesuit
Communications**

Exploring the Treasures of Vatican II
Copyright © 2011 by James H. Kroeger

Claretian Publications is a pastoral endeavor of the Claretian Missionaries in the Philippines. Contact: Claretian Communications Foundation, Inc.; U.P.P.O. Box 4, Diliman; 1101 Quezon City, Philippines; Tel: 921-3984; Fax: 921-6205; cci@claret.org; www.claretianpublications.com

Jesuit Communications produces audio-visual and print media for evangelization and education. Contact: Jesuit Communications Foundation, Inc.; Sonolux Building, Ateneo de Manila University; Loyola Heights, Quezon City, Philippines; Tel: 426-5971 to 72; Fax: 426-5970; jcf@admu.edu.ph; www.ignaciana.org/jescom

---

Library of Congress Cataloging-in-Publication Data

Kroeger, James H.
    Exploring the Treasures of Vatican II
        p. x + 198 cm. 14.6 x 22.2
        ISBN: 978-971051189-1

    1. Vatican Council (2nd : 1962-1965). 2. Catholic Church—
    Doctrines. 3. Catholic Church—History—20th Century.
    4. Church Renewal—Catholic Church. 5. Church Union—
    Catholic Church. I. Title. II. Kroeger, James H.

        BX830.1962 K76 2011
        262.52—dc22

CONTENTS

IV. VATICAN II AND THE CHURCH IN ASIA

V. RESOURCES AND REFERENCES

INTRODUCTION

Pope Benedict XVI, on April 20, 2005, the day after his election as Supreme Pontiff of the Roman Catholic Church, addressed a message to the cardinals, the faithful, and all men and women of good will, outlining his vision for his pontificate. He spoke of his determination "to make Christ's light shine out before men and women of today." He also spoke at length about the example of Pope John Paul II and the importance of the Second Vatican Council.

The new Holy Father, himself a participant in the Council, forcefully noted: "Pope John Paul II rightly pointed out the Council as a 'compass' by which to take our bearings in the vast ocean of the third millennium (NMI 57-58).... Also, in his spiritual Testament he noted, 'I am convinced that it will long be granted to the new generations to draw from the treasures that this twentieth-century Council has lavished upon us....' Thus, as I prepare myself for the service that is proper to the Successor of Peter, I also wish to confirm my determination to continue to put the Second Vatican Council into practice, following in the footsteps of my Predecessors and in faithful continuity with the 2000-year tradition of the Church.... As the years have passed, the Conciliar documents have lost none of their timeliness; indeed, their teachings are proving particularly relevant to the new situation of the Church and the current globalized society."

This collection of Vatican II materials, issued to mark the fiftieth anniversary of the opening of the Council (1962-2012), gathers together fourteen pivotal pieces that present an overview of the Council and its impact on local Churches. The materials are grouped into five broad thematic areas. Section One, comprised of one piece by James Kroeger, presents a popular panoramic overview of the Council; Kroeger views the Council as "a marvelous and generous gift" that the Holy Spirit gave to the Church.

Section Two offers three general introductions to the Second Vatican Council. The first presentation by Robert Trisco and Joseph Komonchak, professors at the Catholic University of America in Washington, D.C., offers an extended summary of the Council under four headings: Preparations, Procedures, Periods, and Pronouncements; Komonchak is recognized as the foremost authority on the Council in the English language. Avery Cardinal Dulles, Professor of Religion and Society at Fordham University in New York, captures the key theological-pastoral principles at the heart of the Council; Dulles presents his insights with an attractive clarity of expression. Denis Hurley, Archbishop of Durban, South Africa, was a participant at Vatican II; through his responses to twenty-six questions on a broad range of topics, Hurley invites the reader into an enriching discovery of the dynamics of the Council.

The third section of the book gathers together several pivotal addresses and messages of Vatican II. Here one finds the widely acclaimed opening speech that Pope John XXIII delivered on the first day of the Council (October 11, 1962) in Saint Peter's Basilica. The pope's address (*Gaudet Mater Ecclesia:* Mother Church Rejoices) captures his vision and hopes for a renewed Church, for a Spirit-inspired "new Pentecost." Two documents by the assembled Council Fathers express the Church's solidarity with all humanity; they assert that the concerns of the Council are not limited to internal Church matters, but are at the service of the entire human family. Two short pieces by Pope Paul VI formally conclude the Council deliberations in Rome; yet, they are outward looking as the pope encourages the bishops to "go out and meet humanity and to bring the good news of the gospel of Christ." Paul VI himself labored tirelessly for thirteen years (1965-1978) to implement the Council's renewed vision of the Church.

Section Four brings together three creative essays by Asian authors who seek to assess the impact of Vatican II on the Church in Asia. Francisco Claver, a Jesuit who served as bishop in two Philippine dioceses, evaluates the Council at two distinct moments: twenty and forty years after its close [1985 and 2005 respectively]. Claver concludes that the Church across Asia has genuinely striven "to become a truly participative Church." Julma Neo, a Filipina religious who has served in leadership roles in the Daughters of Charity of Saint Vincent de Paul, asserts that the renewal of religious life in Asia following the Council vision will demand that each consecrated religious become "a *servant* who is both a *mystic* and a *prophet*." Finally, Peter Phan, a Vietnamese priest who is Professor of Catholic Social Thought at Georgetown University in Washington, D.C., chronicles the reception of the Council in Asia; Phan's extensive bibliographical materials are both impressive and deeply appreciated.

The final section of the book is comprised of two contributions by James Kroeger. For those interested persons who wish to delve into the history and flow of the Second Vatican Council, Kroeger provides a brief overview-chronicle of the key events of the Council. The second piece is a popular bibliography of the Council, a helpful piece to anyone wishing to explore Vatican II at greater length and depth. The same author has provided more comprehensive bibliographical materials in other journals and books. These two pieces will prove particularly helpful for all "students" of Vatican II—for their reading, research, and reflection.

As the Church commemorates the fiftieth anniversary of the opening of the Council (1962-2012), it is hoped that these fourteen selected pieces will renew the interest of all Catholics (young and old) to *appreciate* and *appropriate* the riches of Vatican II—for the continued Spirit-inspired renewal of the faithful and their local Churches.

Pope John XXIII's dream for the Council remains eminently valid today—five decades after he initiated the greatest religious event of the past century. Praying in Assisi exactly one week before the opening of the Council in 1962, John XXIII expressed his desire that the bishops would enter "the Council hall of St. Peter's Basilica as the Apostles and the first disciples of Jesus entered into the Cenacle [Upper Room]." In concluding the first session of the Council (December 8, 1962), John XXIII spoke of another desire that "the acts of the Ecumenical Council meet with the generous and loyal response of the faithful."

Pope John XXIII's words capture the sentiments of the editor of this book: may the Council truly be "a new Pentecost." May Catholics deeply integrate the vision of the Church promoted by Pope John, so that there "will dawn that new Pentecost which is the object of our yearning—a Pentecost that will increase the Church's wealth of spiritual strength and extend her maternal influence and saving power to every sphere of human endeavor." Come, Holy Spirit. *Veni, Sancte Spiritus.*

James H. Kroeger, M.M.
Pentecost Sunday 2011

THE SECOND VATICAN COUNCIL
A Marvelous and Generous Gift

James H. Kroeger, M.M.

In autumn 2012 the Church marks the fiftieth anniversary of the opening of the Second Vatican Council (1962-2012), that great gathering of the world's bishops which has been correctly described by ecclesiologist Komonchak as the most important event in the history of the Roman Catholic Church since the Protestant Reformation. Pope John Paul II has called the Council the most important religious event of the twentieth century. This author remembers the Council well, since he was a junior seminarian at the time. And yet, anyone writing about the Council today (five decades after its 1962 opening session), even the most competent theologian or scholar, knows that he is only offering, at best, a small insight into a momentous phenomenon.

This writer will simply offer four brief, popular glimpses into Vatican II. All, whether serious or humorous, are intended to spark the reader's curiosity, interest, and dedication to embark on a personal journey to discover the profound depths of the Council both in itself as well as in the transforming impact that this "new Pentecost" has had on local Churches around the world.

A Council Panorama. On the feast of the conversion of

Saint Paul (January 25, 1959), less than one hundred days after his election, Pope John XXIII announced his plan to summon all the bishops of the world to a universal Council. Many people were surprised that this "caretaker" pope (he was already 77 years old) would undertake such an enormous project. Some thought that the pope was simply convening a Council to complete the unfinished tasks of Vatican I (1869-1870); John XXIII had something else in mind, or rather "in Spirit."

During the preparatory phases, several commissions and secretariats were established by papal *motu proprio*, meaning under the pope's personal authority. These working committees requested suggestions for topics of discussion; over 9,300 proposals were received. The material was indexed and distributed to eleven commissions appointed by John XXIII in June 1960 to draft discussion documents. These groups included bishops, priests, theologians, one layman and no women. The commissions met between November 1960 and June 1962 and produced 70 documents; these, in turn, were reduced to 20 separate texts and submitted to the pope. In July 1962 seven of these documents were circulated among the bishops of the world in preparation for the opening of the Council in October.

On Christmas day 1961 John XXIII had formally summoned the Council with his apostolic constitution *Humanae Salutis*. Vatican II opened on October 11, 1962. One can recall several significant moments of this first session: John XXIII's visionary and programmatic address, *Gaudet Mater Ecclesia* (Mother Church Rejoices); the bishops' refusal to accept the Roman Curia's organization of the conciliar commissions; the debates on the liturgy, revelation, and the Church; the rejection of the Curia's draft document on the Church. New winds were obviously blowing through the Church.

"Good Pope John" died on June 3, 1963; he was succeeded by Paul VI who announced his firm intention to continue the Council. Paul VI's address at the opening of the second session (September 29) listed four aims: the development of a deeper idea of the Church, its renewal, the unity of all Christians, and dialogue between the Church and the world. At the end of this second session (December 4), the first two Council documents were formally approved (Sacred Liturgy and Social Communication).

In the eight-month interval between Council sessions, Paul VI took some key initiatives: he visited Ecumenical Patriarch Athenagoras in the Holy Land (January 1964); on Pentecost Sunday (May 1964) he established the Secretariat for Non-Christians [renamed in 1988 the Pontifical Council for Interreligious Dialogue]; in August he issued his first encyclical letter, *Ecclesiam Suam*; over half of this document focused on "dialogue" as an important key to the identity of the Church.

The third session of the Council extended from September 14 until November 21, 1964. There were discussions on a wide variety of complex topics: religious liberty, the Jews, the laity, the Church in the modern world, marriage, culture, the missions, and the formation of priests. Three documents were issued (The Church, Eastern Catholic Churches, and Ecumenism).

The intervening months between the third and fourth Council sessions witnessed some important events: Paul VI attended the Eucharistic Congress in India (November 1964); Cardinal Bea visited the World Council of Churches in Geneva (February 1965); Paul VI publicly celebrated Mass in the vernacular on the very first day it was permitted (March 1965); Paul VI issued his encyclical letter *Mysterium Fidei* (September 1965).

The fourth and final session of the Council began on

September 14, 1965. The very next day Paul VI established the long-awaited Synod of Bishops. The Council Fathers debated the documents on the missions, religious life, priestly formation, priestly life and ministry, and non-Christian religions. Much of this session was devoted to a careful discussion of the document on the Church in the Modern World. Eleven more documents were issued, four of which bear the date December 7, 1965, the final public session of the Council. The closing ceremony was held in Saint Peter's Square on December 8, 1965. The sixteen Council documents include: four Constitutions, nine Decrees, and three Declarations. The official Latin texts, exclusive of 992 footnotes of varying length, run to approximately 103,014 words. A phenomenal achievement!

Startling Statistics. While recognizing that the significance of the Second Vatican Council is to be found in its sixteen documents as well as in the renewal of the Church wrought by the action of the Holy Spirit, one may enjoy looking at some of the "impressive" facts of the entire Vatican II project.

Vatican Radio statistically summed up the Council in five sentences. There were 168 general meetings and 10 plenary ones; the first session had 36 general meetings, the second 43, the third 48, and the last 41. During the general meetings there were 147 introductions or reports read and 2,212 speeches; there were also 4,361 written interventions. The average daily attendance of bishops was 2,200; the peak of 2,392 was reached on December 6, 1965. During the period of the sessions, 242 Council Fathers died, including 12 cardinals. The number of officially designated experts was 460, of whom 235 were diocesan priests, 45 were Jesuits, 42 Dominicans, and 15 Franciscans.

Additional fascinating statistics (with some minor vari-ations) are given by Ralph Wiltgen, SVD. The total cost to the Vatican for the Council and its preparatory work was $7,250,000.00. Since 2,860 Council Fathers attended all or part of the four sessions, which stretched over 281 days, the average outlay was $2,530 per Council Father, or $9 per day. These costs, however, did not include the expenses borne by the Council Fathers themselves; 67% paid their own transportation costs, and 53% paid for their own lodging. Of the total spent by the Vatican, 33% was used for lodging; 30% for transportation; 9% for furnishing the Council hall; 8% for the combined expenses of computers, Council Press Office, printing jobs, and telephone installations; 20% went for other costs.

Sickness, old age, or government-imposed restrictions prevented 274 Council Fathers from attending. Between the opening and closing dates, 253 Council Fathers died, and 296 new ones were added. Of the 98 cardinals who took part, 11 died before the Council was over; the only cardinal not in attendance was Josef Cardinal Mindszenty of Hungary. The average age of the Council Fathers was 60. Two-thirds were secular clergy, and the rest were members of religious orders.

The records of the Council are contained in two hundred large volumes that have the alphabetical lists of Council Fathers, indicating how each one voted on all 544 ballots. In addition to having all the documents on file, the archives contain a complete magnetic tape recording of all 168 general congregations, filling 712 reels, each 1,300 feet long, which run for 542 hours. Pope Paul VI praised the General Secretariat of the Council for its work in providing a complete theological, organizational, and administrative record of the Council. Statistics do not tell the full story of the Council, but they certainly reveal another rich dimension of John XXIII's ambitious project.

A Church Renewed. The term that Pope John XXIII employed to capture his agenda for the Council was *aggiornamento,* an Italian term which means a "bringing up to date"; the term has almost become synonymous with the Church renewal fostered by Vatican II. It is reminiscent of the Latin phrase *ecclesia semper reformanda,* the Church must always be reforming; she always needs renewal, revitalization, transformation, conversion, change, and growth. John XXIII and the Vatican Council itself desired such a genuine renewal, under the lead of the Holy Spirit, so that the Church could more deeply discover her true identity and more effectively accomplish her mission in the contemporary world.

The general aims of renewal sought by the Council were enunciated at the beginning of the very first document issued by the Council, the Constitution on the Sacred Liturgy: "It is the goal of this most sacred Council to intensify the daily growth of Catholics in Christian living; to make more responsive to the requirements of our times those Church institutions which are open to change; to nurture whatever can contribute to the unity of all who believe in Christ; and, to strengthen those aspects of the Church which can help summon all humanity into her embrace" (SC 1). Indeed, a comprehensive, wide-ranging transformation was envisioned.

This *aggiornamento* was not focused primarily on the change of external structures; John XXIII envisioned a profound inner transformation. External changes would naturally flow from a deep interior renewal. This vision is captured well in the chapter on "The Universal Call to Holiness," the fifth chapter of *Lumen Gentium.* "Therefore in the Church, everyone … is called to holiness…. This holiness of the Church is unceasingly manifested, as it ought to be, through those fruits of grace which the Spirit produces in the faithful…. Thus, it is evident to everyone that all the faithful of Christ of whatever rank or status are called to the fullness of the Christian life…."

One individual who distinctly contributed to fostering the comprehensive renewal of the Church during the Council was Leo Josef Cardinal Suenens; his crucial role was to provide direction for the Council in its earliest days. Suenens outlined a simple framework to guide the Council; he proposed that the central theme would be the Church as such, understood in its *ad intra* (internal) and *ad extra* (external) dimensions. In fact, the Council did ultimately provide a providential clarification of the true nature of the Church, so that knowing her own identity, she might more effectively serve all humanity as *sacramentum mundi,* the sacrament of the world.

A careful examination of the sixteen documents of Vatican II reveals how they serve this two-fold renewal of all the "inner" and "outer" dimensions of the Church. The Council documents actually form a kind of "network" that touches the interior life of the Church (e.g. liturgy, bishops, religious, priests, etc.) as well as its external dimensions (e.g. mission, church in the modern world, religions, religious freedom, etc.). Of course, both aspects are interrelated and concomitantly enhance each other. Truly, the renewal project of the Council was marvellously comprehensive in its scope. In addition, from the beginning, the bishops recognized that their task was not just updating current Church practices; the renewal demanded a process of *ressourcement,* returning to the sources of the faith and integrating them into contemporary ecclesiology.

The renewal sought by John XXIII in his *aggiornamento* agenda resulted in numerous transformations in the Church; however, the most significant achievement is the renewed biblical understanding of the Church as People of God, Body of Christ, and Temple of the Spirit as well as Sacrament to the World. The deep transformations that the Council set in motion continue to reverberate throughout the Church. Indeed, the Council is, in the image of Popes John Paul II and Benedict

XVI, the "compass" that continues to guide the Church on her pilgrim path.

At the final session of the Council, Pope Paul VI offered an insightful definition of Pope John XXIII's pivotal watchword: "From now on *aggiornamento* will signify for us a widely undertaken quest for a deeper understanding of the spirit of the Council and the faithful application of the norms it has happily and prayerfully provided." These relevant words continue to challenge Catholics to receive and implement the marvelous and generous gift of the Spirit in Vatican II.

"Genius of the Heart." During his lifetime Pope John XXIII was immensely popular with people from all walks of life; he was often given various "titles." He was known as "The People's Pope" and as "Good Pope John." When he died on June 3, 1963 (Pentecost Monday) a major newspaper headline simply read: "A Death in the Family." Since his beatification on September 3, 2000, he is "Blessed Pope John." His incorrupt body can now be viewed through an etched glass-faced coffin near the main nave of Saint Peter's Basilica.

This writer prefers to give another title to John XXIII, calling him a "Genius of the Heart." He lived and loved life—to the full. An easy-going man, he enjoyed people, stopping to talk, for example, with the gardeners while on a stroll. He invited the new recruits of the Swiss Guard to have a drink with him so he could get to know them. He spent his first Christmas as pope with the sick in two Roman hospitals; the next day he visited the prisoners at Rome's *Regina Coeli* prison. He had known the horrors of World War I, having been drafted into the military as a chaplain. His deep faith and prayer-life were evident; he prayed the fifteen decades of the rosary daily. He was a "Good Shepherd" who knew people's hearts; he was a "Genius of the Heart."

Everyone loved Pope John's wit, his zest for life. He possessed in abundance a quality exceptional in a pope—a hearty sense of humor. A few incidents and quotes reveal this dimension of the "Father of Vatican II."

A newly accredited diplomat to the Vatican was received by the Pope and he asked: "How many persons work at the Vatican?" John XXIII replied with a wink in his eye: "Oh, no more than half of them." On another occasion, when the Pope was preparing to meet President and Mrs. Kennedy, he asked a monsignor what proper protocol would be; several suggestions were given (e.g. Madame). However, when he entered the audience room, he spontaneously opened his arms, smiled broadly, and exclaimed: "Ah, Jacqueline!" When the Pope visited the Holy Spirit hospital in Rome, he met the Mother Superior who said: "Most Holy Father, I am the Superior of the Holy Spirit." "Well, I must say you're lucky," replied the Pope. "I'm only the Vicar of Jesus Christ!"

During processions the Pope was often carried on the *sedia gestatoria* (portable chair) so the crowds could see him better. John XXIII found it distasteful, saying that it made him dizzy; he protested: "This is the most uncomfortable chair I know!" On one occasion he overheard two Italian women speaking of his appearance; they said he looked ugly; he was so fat and his nose so huge. The Pope quipped to them: "Being Pope is not a beauty contest!"

When he was Apostolic Nuncio to France, the future pope was asked during a dinner party: "Are you embarrassed, Monsignor, when there are women present who wear very low-necked dresses? It's often a scandal." Msgr. Roncalli replied: "A scandal? Why, no! When there's a woman with a plunging neckline, the guests don't look at her. They look at the Apostolic Nuncio to see how he is taking it."

John XXIII spoke of the Council on various occasions. "The Council?" he said as he moved towards a window, gesturing as if to open it. "I expect a little fresh air from it.... We must shake off the imperial dust that has accumulated on the throne of Saint Peter since Constantine." John's intentions were clear: "We desire above all that the Council be an act of goodness." There would be no condemnations during the Council, because today the Church must prefer "the balm of mercy to the arm of severity." When a concerned prelate of the Curia told the Pope that it was absolutely impossible to open the Council in 1963, he replied: "Fine, we'll open it in 1962!"

Pope John confessed that he had some difficulty in falling asleep on the night after he announced the Council. He said that he talked to himself in this way: "Giovanni, why don't you sleep? Is it the Pope or the Holy Spirit who governs the Church? It's the Holy Spirit, no? Well, then, go to sleep, Giovanni!" Once, during the first session of the Council, he quipped: "I would like very much for Our Lord to appear to me to tell me when the Council will end. To get it started, I am in command, but to finish it...." On the evening of the opening day of the Council in 1962, the Pope addressed the Romans assembled in Saint Peter's Square: "When you go back to your homes, hug your children for me. Tell them that it is an affectionate embrace from the Pope." Without doubt, people around the world found a special place in their heart for John XXIII; he was the loveable and compassionate man, who now, as "Blessed Pope John," intercedes for us.

Concluding Reflection. As the Church celebrates the fiftieth anniversary of the opening of the Council (1962-2012), she needs to assess the impact of Vatican II. A key question to be asked is focused on the "reception" of the Council. How have the vision and the experience of the Council changed and renewed the local Churches—particularly in Asia? Has the "rush of the Spirit" been felt deeply, changing people's awareness, attitudes, and behavior? Where are we five decades after John XXIII began his program of *aggiornamento*? What are the new pathways of the Spirit we Catholics are challenged to discern and travel today—all in fidelity to the Council?

SECOND VATICAN ECUMENICAL COUNCIL
A Synthetic Overview

R. Trisco and J. Komonchak

This lengthy presentation provides an extended summary of the Second Vatican Ecumenical Council. Following a short introduction, the material is unfolded in four major sections: **I.** Preparatory Commissions; **II.** Rules and Procedures; **III.** Periods [Council Sessions: 1962-1965]; and, **IV.** Pronouncements of the Council.

Introduction. On January 25, 1959, less than one hundred days after his election, in a speech in which he outlined the broad lines of his papacy, Pope John XXIII told a group of cardinals gathered at Saint Paul-Outside-the-Walls that he intended to revive two ancient forms for stating doctrine and ordering discipline: he would hold a diocesan synod for Rome and an ecumenical council for the universal Church. The two events would be followed by a reform of the Code of Canon Law. The announcement of a council surprised most Catholics. No ecumenical council had been held since the First Vatican Council, and some churchmen were of the view that its definitions of papal primacy and infallibility made further ecumenical councils superfluous. Both Pius XI and Pius XII had considered reconvening Vatican I, but although consultations were undertaken and some considerations of an agenda were begun, in the end both popes decided not to proceed.

In various speeches and messages over the next years, John XXIII set out three general purposes for the Council: (1) he wished it to be an opportunity for a spiritual renewal and reinvigoration of the Church that would make it more faithful to Christ's will and (2) for an updating (*aggiornamento*) of its pastoral attitudes, habits, and institutions to make them more effective in the changed conditions of the modern world. If these two goals could be achieved, the Council would also (3) greatly promote the restoration of unity among Christians.

I. Preparatory Commissions. On Pentecost Sunday, May 17, 1959, the pope established an Antepreparatory Commission headed by Cardinal Tardini, with Monsignor Pericle Felici serving as secretary, and composed of ten clerics who held important posts in the Roman Curia. This commission's tasks were to consult the bishops of the world, the offices of the Curia, and the theological and canonical faculties of Catholic universities for their advice and suggestions about a conciliar agenda. They were also to sketch the general lines of the topics to be discussed at the Council and to suggest various bodies that would prepare the material for conciliar deliberation. The bishops and others consulted were left complete freedom to make suggestions in the areas of doctrine, discipline, pastoral activity, and contemporary problems. Over 75% of those invited responded; their responses filled fifteen large tomes in four volumes. Proposals ranged in significance from the sublime to the trivial and reflected a very broad range of theological and pastoral perspectives; there were those who opposed any change and those who hoped the Council would be an opportunity for major reforms. If the majority of bishops were rather cautious and earth-bound in their suggestions, it could have been in part because of the deadline for their submissions, and also in part because it was not at all clear what Pope John himself wished the Council to be and to do.

In the vast material received, the antepreparatory commission found no fewer than 9,338 suggestions which it organized for convenient reference according to the traditional divisions of dogmatic and moral theology and also according to the books and topics of the Code of Canon Law. The proposals received were placed under the seal of secrecy and could be consulted only by those officially engaged in the preparation of the Council. As the structure of the preparation took shape, the materials were divided once again, drastically reduced in number, and presented in the form of questions for further study.

On Pentecost, June 5, 1960, John XXIII announced the structure of the preparatory period. Ten commissions were established to draw up texts for the Council to consider: (1) for matters of faith and morals (the theological); (2) for bishops and the governance of dioceses; (3) for the discipline of the clergy and the Christian people; (4) for religious; (5) for the discipline of the sacraments; (6) for the liturgy; (7) for studies and seminaries; (8) for the eastern churches; (9) for the missions; (10) for the apostolate of the laity. In addition, the pope created two secretariats, one for the communications-media and the other for promoting the unity of Christians which, it was said, would enable non-Catholics to follow the work of the Council. A Central Commission was also established to supervise and coordinate the work of the other commissions, to review the texts they prepared and recommend them to the pope for the conciliar agenda, and to draw up the rules that would govern the Council's work.

The ten commissions were chaired by the cardinal-heads of corresponding offices in the Roman Curia, with Curial figures also serving as secretaries on most of them. The personnel of the commissions consisted of members and consultors, the former having voting rights, the latter offering advice when asked. Among the members and consultors, it was noted, were some theologians who had been under suspicion or the subject of disciplinary measures during the previous decade, among them Yves Congar, Henri de Lubac, Bernard Häring, and Karl Rahner. No women and no lay people were appointed to the preparatory commissions.

The commissions set to work on the basis of the questions proposed by the antepreparatory commission, although they were permitted to suggest additional questions. The work of preparation suffered from a lack of supervision and from the failure of the most of the commissions to collaborate on common or related problems. The Theological Commission, headed by Alfredo Cardinal Ottaviani, added to the problem by insisting that it had exclusive responsibility for doctrinal questions. As it would not enter into practical pastoral problems, so it expected all other commissions to submit to itself any and all matters of doctrine. In further expression of its conception of its own sovereignty, the Theological Commission refused to collaborate with other commissions and in particular with the Secretariat for Christian Unity. Compounding this lack of coordination, the pontifical secrecy that was supposed to surround the work of the commissions was widely understood to prohibit speaking about the work of one's own commission, even with members of other commissions.

The commissions brought before the Central Commission a total of 75 texts which were later culled, some remanded to the postconciliar reform of canon law, some combined with others, so that a total of 22 Schemas were in the end considered fit for conciliar discussion. The texts prepared by the pastoral commissions generally flew very close to the ground; they did little more than recommend mostly minor changes in the Church's canonical and disciplinary norms; there was very little evidence that the commissions had considered the serious sociological and theological discussions of pastoral activity that had been going on for three decades. The one exception to this description was the Commission on the Sacred Liturgy whose members included many of the most important scholars in the liturgical movement; they decided to undertake serious historical and theological studies of the various topics they addressed and were therefore able to buttress with effective arguments their recommendations of significant liturgical reform.

The Theological Commission prepared eight texts: a new formula for the profession of faith, meant to be used at the opening of the Council, and seven constitutions: (1) on the sources of revelation, (2) on the moral order, (3) on defending the deposit of faith, (4) on chastity, virginity, marriage and the family, (5) on the Church, (6) on the Blessed Virgin Mary, and (7) on the community of nations and the social order. In general, these texts were meant to confirm with the Council's high authority the orientations and emphases that had characterized the papal magisterium for the previous century and a half, in particular as these had been expressed at Vatican I, in the anti-modernist documents, *Pascendi* and *Lamentabili,* and in the encyclical *Humani Generis.* Their general tone was very defensive, suspicious of most of the recent movements of theological renewal in dogmatic and moral theology and in biblical studies, and at best indifferent to ecumenical implications.

During the preparatory period the Secretariat for Christian Unity, chaired by Cardinal Augustin Bea, represented a different notion of what the Council might do and how it might do it. Early on, it received permission from Pope John to prepare texts to alert the other commissions to the ecumenical dimensions of various subjects. When its efforts to collaborate with the Theological Commission were rebuffed, it began to prepare texts that the Pope said could eventually be brought to the Council itself. Some of the Secretariat's texts addressed questions being considered also by the Theological Commission, among them the Word of God, membership in the Church, hierarchical authority, and religious freedom. These texts were written with an eye to overcoming misunderstandings of Catholic doctrine on the part of other Christians, to exploring their views with sympathy, and to proposing ways of understanding and stating Christian doctrine that would go beyond polemical impasses.

All of the texts written by the preparatory commissions were brought for review before the Central Commission, which was composed of cardinals and archbishops from all over the world and which met in six meetings between June 12, 1961, and June 20, 1962. The members of this commission were not reluctant to criticize the prepared texts and to offer amendments. Had people been aware of the quality and vigor of the discussions within the Central Commission, the public might have anticipated the drama that unfolded when some of these texts reached the Council floor. The criticisms and proposed amendments were referred to a subcommission whose work was then to be reviewed by the whole Central Commission; time did not permit this last step and consequently the texts went before the Council as altered or not by the subcommission.

II. **Rules and Procedures.** By the *motu proprio Appropinquante Concilio* (August 6, 1962) John XXIII laid down the rules that were to govern the conduct of the Council. For the direction of the general congregations, in which the proposed decrees were to be discussed and voted on, he established a board of ten presidents, all cardinals, who were to supervise the debate and maintain discipline, one of them presiding each day. He also set up ten commissions, which were the same as those in the preparatory phase, although the first was now called the Commission for the Doctrine of Faith and Morals, and the last was now charged with matters pertaining not only to the apostolate of the laity but also to mass media and entertainment. The Secretariat for Promoting Christian Unity, the Technical-

Organizational Commission, and the Financial Secretariat were carried over, and at the last minute the Pope added a Secretariat for Extraordinary Affairs which would examine new questions proposed by the fathers.   Besides the chairman, who was named by the pope, each conciliar commission consisted of 24 members, two-thirds of whom were elected by the fathers and the rest chosen by the pope; this represented a change from Vatican I where all the members of the conciliar commissions were elected by the assembly.   Latin was to be used in the public sessions and general congregations; modern languages could also be used in commission meetings.   The speeches of individual fathers were not to last more than ten minutes.   The majority required for approval of all matters except elections consisted of two-thirds of those present and voting.   Some of these provisions would be later modified in the light of the conciliar experience.

On July 23, 1962, the General Secretariat of the Council, with Archbishop Pericle Felici continuing at its head, sent the conciliar fathers a first volume containing the texts that would be discussed at the first session of the Second Vatican Council.   It contained the following draft texts: (1) on dogmatic constitutions on the sources of revelation, (2) on the defense of the deposit of faith, (3) on the Christian moral order, (4) on chastity, marriage, the family and virginity, (5) on the sacred liturgy, (6) on the mass media, and (7) on the unity of the Church (dealing with the Oriental Catholic Churches).   Why out of the mass of material prepared these seven texts were chosen for the initial conciliar agenda is not known.   That the draft of a dogmatic constitution on the Church and on the Blessed Virgin Mary was not included was explained by the fact that the final revisions and editing of these two texts were not completed when the Council opened. A second volume would be distributed to the fathers only early in November.

The ecumenical goal of the Council was reflected by invitations sent to the major Christian churches and communities. Their representatives were permitted to attend not only the public sessions but also the general congregations, but they did not have the right to vote or to speak; they would prove able, however, to make their views known to the commissions through the Secretariat for Christian Unity and through personal contacts with conciliar fathers. It was a great disappointment that most of the Orthodox Churches were not represented at the first session, but a decision made at a pan-Orthodox meeting in Rhodes in 1961 had decided upon a common response. On the very eve of the Council, however, the Moscow patriarchate broke with the rest and decided to send representatives. The representatives of the Patriarch of Constantinople would not attend the Council until the third session. Ecumenical representation at the Council increased from year to year; 17 Orthodox and Protestant denominations were represented by 35 delegate-observers and guests at the first period, while at the fourth period 93 represented 28 groups.

The announcement of the Council and the years of its preparation had created widespread interest both within and without the Catholic Church. A spate of historical surveys and studies of the previous 20 ecumenical councils appeared, along with monographs on topics likely to be discussed at Vatican II, particularly in the areas of liturgy and ecclesiology. Surveys of the desires and wishes of Catholics with regard to the Council were published, and several authors' published proposals for a reform agenda.

In the spring of 1962, several important members of the Central Commission, among them Cardinals Suenens (Malines-Brussels) and Léger (Montreal) and Archbishop Denis Hurley (Durban, South Africa) [see chapter containing his interview in 2000], wrote to Pope John to express their concern that the pastoral and ecumenical goals he had outlined for the Council were unlikely to be met on the basis of the texts the Central Commission had reviewed. Such fears spread as the character of the official texts became more widely known. There was some apprehension that the Council, which was not expected to last more than two sessions, would entail little more than rubberstamping the documents placed before the fathers. As the bishops began to gather in Rome in the second week of October 1962, contrasting fears and hopes divided them.

III.   Periods. The Second Vatican Council met in four periods or sessions: from October 11 to December 8, 1962; from September 29 to December 4, 1963; from September 14 to November 21, 1964; and, from September 14 to December 8, 1965.

In the course of the four years of Vatican II, 3,058 fathers participated, by far the largest number in the history of the ecumenical councils. Besides the 129 superiors general of clerical religious orders, their numbers and the percentages of all those who attended, ranked by continent, are: Europe 1,060 (36%); South America 531 (18%); North America 416 (14%); Asia 408 (14%); Africa 351 (12%); Central America 89 (3%); and Oceania 74 (3%). Participation by those who had a right to attend fluctuated. It was the highest at the first (84.34%) and at the fourth (84.88%) periods; 82.34% attended the second and 80.23% the third. These numbers would have been higher had many bishops from countries under Communist domination been permitted to attend.

A.   First Period. The most dramatic of the four periods of the Council opened with a solemn ceremony attended by representatives of 86 governments and international bodies. In his opening speech Pope John disagreed with "those prophets of doom who are always forecasting disaster" and recommended that the fathers instead consider whether God might not be providing new opportunities for the Church. He wanted the Council not only to defend the patrimony of the faith but to also consider how to understand and present it to contemporaries; to this end he distinguished between the substance of the faith and the fashion in which it is articulated, and he urged a pastoral goal and the use of the methods of research and literary forms of modern thought. In the face of errors he advised the fathers to avoid condemnations and instead to give a positive demonstration of the validity of the Church's teaching. He emphasized the duty to work actively for the fulfilment of the mystery of unity with other Christians and with non-Christians. To those familiar with the preparatory material, it appeared that the pope was declaring his dissatisfaction with the official schemata and proposing that the Council adopt a different approach [see special chapter for John XXIII's opening speech].

The first general congregation (October 13, 1962) had permanent consequences for the Council, for instead of proceeding immediately, as had been planned, to electing the 16 members of each commission with only the lists of members and consultors of the defunct preparatory commissions to guide it, the Council, at the motion of Cardinal Achille Liénart (Lille) and of Cardinal Josef Frings (Cologne), adjourned after a few minutes to allow more time for consultation among the bishops of the various countries or regions. Thereupon, the national or regional episcopal conferences decided to recommend one or two candidates of their own number for each commission. In the second general congregation (October 16), before the fathers cast their ballots, a composite list of all these nominees was distributed. In this way the commissions became more nearly representative of the whole assembly and did not merely perpetuate the mentality of the preparatory commissions, which had been largely dominated by curialists and could have been expected merely to defend texts which many fathers considered to be unacceptable. Continuity was assured, however, by the pope's appointment as presidents of the conciliar commissions some of the same curial cardinals who had presided over the corresponding preparatory commissions. The postponement of these elections was a first indication that the fathers were going to accept their responsibility for the Council, and the consultations undertaken established the importance for the Council of cooperation within and among the episcopal conferences.

In the course of this first period the Council discussed the schemata on the liturgy, on the sources of revelation, on mass media, on the unity of the Church, and on the Church. Lively discussions took place on the liturgical schema's proposals to allow greater use of vernacular languages, more common practice of communion under both kinds and concelebration, and greater authority in liturgical matters for episcopal conferences. The long debate came to a close with a vote on the general principles set out in the draft. An overwhelming majority of the fathers (2,162 to 46) showed themselves ready to embark upon significant Church reform.

The second important debate concerned a schema on the sources of revelation which focused on two questions: the relationship between Scripture and Tradition and the value of modern historical critical methods in the interpretation of the Bible. The text was sharply criticized for its negative tone and lack of ecumenical and pastoral sensitivity, for prematurely settling the legitimately debated issue whether all revealed truths are found in the Scriptures, and for looking with such suspicion on the problems uncovered by modern biblical scholarship that it would prevent any fruitful Catholic contribution. Defenders of the text argued that the dogmatic issue had been settled at the Council of Trent and by subsequent common teaching and that the faith was being endangered by books and articles calling into question the historical character of both Old and

New Testaments. A vote was taken on whether to discontinue the debate or to continue it with discussions of the individual chapters. Although the vote to discontinue (1,368 to 822) fell just short of the two-thirds majority required, the pope, to avoid prolonged and probably fruitless debate, intervened, halting the discussion and remanding the text to a special commission under the joint chairmanship of Cardinals Ottaviani and Bea to rewrite the text. It had become clear that a substantial majority of the fathers wished to compose texts different in orientation and purpose from those composed by the Theological Commission, and that the pope would back them up.

Now that the Council had clearly demonstrated its pastoral and doctrinal interests, the rest of the first period was somewhat anticlimactic. A few days were given at the end to a preliminary discussion of the schema on the Church, commonly considered the chief business and central theme of the whole Council. The official text was subjected to a by now familiar litany of complaints, and it was understood, even without a formal vote, that it too would have to be substantially revised. In fact, that would prove to be the fate of all the prepared schemata. On December 6, 1962, it was announced that the Pope had appointed a Coordinating Commission, chaired by Cardinal Amleto Cicognani, whose task it would be to review the draft texts prepared for the Council, and, in the light of the goals of the Council as stated by Pope John and ratified by the Council's votes, to decide which were to be retained on the conciliar agenda, which could be left for post-conciliar decisions, and what changes in content, method, or tone needed to be made. This "supercommission" rapidly reduced the texts to be retained to 17, the last of these being a new schema, championed in particular by Cardinal Suenens, to address the presence of the Church in the modern world. Throughout the intersession, the conciliar commissions undertook what has been called a "second preparation" of Vatican II.

The first period ended without its having approved a single schema, but the decisions made at it determined the orientation of the whole course of the Second Vatican Council. The people and the purposes that had largely dominated the preparation of the Council had been replaced; new leaders would now pursue goals largely ignored during the preparation.

With the death of John XXIII on June 3, 1963, the Council and all activities related to it were automatically suspended. But, the day after his election (June 22), Pope Paul VI promised that the Council would be resumed and that it would pursue the goals set for it by his predecessor. Five days later he fixed the opening date of the second period for September 29.

B. Second Period. Before the fathers reconvened, Paul VI issued a revised edition of the *Ordo Concilii … celebrandi* in order to correct some of the defects in organization and procedure manifested in the first period and to expedite the labors and ensure the freedom of the participants. He abolished the Secretariat for Extraordinary Affairs and enlarged to 12 members the board of presidents; it would be their duty to see that the rules were duly observed and to resolve any eventual doubts and remove difficulties. He also appointed four cardinals Agagianian, Prefect of the Congregation de Propaganda Fide; Giacomo Lercaro (Bologna); Julius Döpfner (Munich and Freising); and Leo Joseph Suenens (Malines-Brussels) as moderators, who were to take turns in directing the discussions in the general congregations. The pope also made various changes in the procedural rules, such as reducing to 50 percent plus one the majority required for the rejection or deferment of a schema or a part of one, and permitting one father to speak in the name of others.

For the improvement and expansion of the news ser-vices, about which there had been many complaints during the first period, Paul VI appointed a Press Committee chaired by Archbishop Martin J. O'Connor. The pope increased the number of non-Catholic Christian observers invited to the Council, and 31 more were present at the second period than at the first. John XXIII had invited one Catholic layman, Jean Guitton, to the latter part of the first period; Paul VI provided for the attendance of several lay auditors at the general congregations and for their assistance to the commissions; in addition to Guitton, ten other laymen from various countries, for the most part representing international Catholic organizations, were welcomed at the start of the new period.

At the public session which opened the second period on September 29, 1963, Paul VI gave a memorable address in which he emphasized the pastoral nature of the assembly and specified its four purposes: (1) to define more fully the notion of the Church, especially with regard to the position of bishops; (2) to renew the Church; (3) to promote the restoration of unity among all Christians [he asked for non-Catholics to pardon Catholics for their faults in the schisms and condoned injuries done to Catholics]; and, (4) to initiate a dialogue with the contemporary world.

The conciliar discussions began with the revised schema on the Church. Heated debate arose over the schema's discussion of the collegiality of bishops and its relation to the primacy of the pope defined at Vatican I. On October 30, the moderators, employing a procedure not envisaged in the *Ordo*, put to votes for the guidance of the Doctrinal Commission five propositions contained substantially in the schema's third chapter. Four of them concerned the sacramentality of the episcopate and its collegial character and authority; the fifth concerned the restoration of the diaconate as a permanent order. All five of the propositions received majorities of more than two-thirds, thus removing all doubts about the progressive tendency of the Council. But the "irregular" character of the votes would be evoked many times afterward to call into question their validity.

Also in connection with the schema on the Church, another division among the fathers appeared over the question whether the schema on the Blessed Virgin Mary should be a separate text or be incorporated into the schema on the Church. After an emotional debate, the question was put to a vote on October 29, and by the narrowest margin in all the Council's deliberations (1,114 to 1,074) the assembly decide to incorporate it into the constitution on the Church.

During a discussion of the schema on bishops and the governance of dioceses (November 5-15), one of the Council's rare dramatic confrontations occurred when Cardinal Frings frankly criticized the methods of the Holy Office; Cardinal Ottaviani, its secretary, vehemently defended them. The first three chapters of the schema on ecumenism were discussed (November 18 - December 2) and were approved on condition of revision, but, to the consternation of many fathers, all action on the fourth chapter (on the Church's attitude toward non-Christians and especially the Jews) and on the fifth (on religious freedom) was deferred to the third period, allegedly because of lack of time for mature consideration.

On November 21 the pope announced that the number of members of each commission would be increased to 30. After the episcopal conferences again nominated candidates, the fathers elected the greater part of the new members on November 28, and the pope appointed the rest. The commissions then elected a new additional vice-chairman and secretary. The avowed purpose of these changes was to expedite the labors of the commissions, but they seem also to have been intended to help bring some recalcitrant commissions into greater harmony with the wishes of the conciliar majority.

During a ceremony commemorating the conclusion of the Council of Trent (December 3), Paul VI made known his *motu proprio Pastorale Munus* (November 30), in which he either granted or declared to be restored (his language was ambiguous) to bishops certain faculties and privileges, many of which had been proposed in an appendix to the schema on bishops and the government of dioceses. The relatively insignificant character of many of these faculties or privileges underscored in the minds of many fathers and observers the degree to which the episcopate had in the past become dependent upon the papacy.

On December 4, the concluding public session of the second period was held. The fathers definitively passed the constitution on the liturgy by a vote of 2,147 to 4 and, by a vote of 1,980 to 164, the decree on the communications media. Against the latter decree, opposition had been raised at the last minute on the grounds that it would not answer the expectation of Christians and would compromise the Council's authority; the final vote in a general congregation on November 25 had seen over 500 bishops vote against it. The pope, using a formula that stressed his union with the other conciliar fathers, approved and promulgated the two texts, the first of the final documents of the Council. On January 25, 1964, he issued the *motu proprio Sacram Liturgiam* by which he established a commission for the implementation of the liturgical constitution.

In his closing address Paul VI thanked those fathers who had contributed toward the expenses of the Council or had aided their needy brothers, remarked that the Council had been marked by assiduous labor and freedom of expression, expressed the hope that it could complete its work in a third period, and announced his forthcoming pilgrimage to the Holy Land.

During the interval between the second and third periods the fathers were again invited to submit further comments on the unfinished business, and with the help of this counsel the commissions continued to revise the schemata. At the direction of the Coordinating Commission and in accord with the pope's own desires, they reduced some of the topics, namely, those on priests, religious, education for the priesthood, missionary activity, marriage, and Catholic education, to a series of brief and basic principles on which the fathers would be expected to agree easily and quickly, and without public discussion, in the third period; the fuller articulation and implementation of these principles could be left to postconciliar bodies. This reduction of the conciliar agenda, known as the "Döpfner plan," was designed to ensure that the Council could end its work with the third session, and in furtherance of this purpose changes were made also in the conciliar procedures to prevent repetitions and to expedite decisions.

Just before the third period was to open, the pope announced that women would now join the lay men as auditors of the Council. Among the increased number of observer-delegates, for the first time, were representatives of the Patriarchate of Constantinople.

C. Third Period. Pope Paul opened the third period on September 14, 1964, with a public session at which he concelebrated Mass with 24 conciliar fathers, a first conciliar expression of the concrete reforms approved in the constitution on the liturgy at the end of the second period. The conciliar discussions began with chapters of the schema on the Church not yet approved in general and then with successive votes on the eight chapters as amended. In the discussion of the chapter on the Blessed Virgin Mary, debate focused on whether to accord her the titles "Mediatrix" and "Mother of the Church." Very great interest attended the votes on the third chapter, on the hierarchical constitution of the Church with special reference to bishops. The battle over the relationship between papal primacy and episcopal collegiality had not grown less fierce, and in fact, on the very eve of the third period, Paul VI had received a confidential note from prominent cardinals and heads of religious orders begging him not to allow the teaching of the chapter to be voted on and not very subtly implying that if he did not so act, he would be guilty of squandering the authority of his office. After four formal reports on the chapter were read out to the assembly, the voting did proceed, and on the major issues under debate the votes were overwhelmingly favorable.

Discussions followed on the schema on the pastoral office of bishops whose progress, however, was impeded by the need to await the results of the voting on the schema on the Church. The schemas on religious freedom and on the Jews, which had originally been part of the schema on ecumenism, were now to become distinct documents; the debate on them was vigorous and was marked by concerns both theological and political. The text on religious freedom was criticized for departing from the Church's traditional insistence on the unique rights of the true religion; it was defended as reflecting the development of political realities, respecting the dignity and freedom of persons, and a prerequisite for any serious ecumenical or interreligious dialogue. The schema on the Church's relationship with Jews continued to receive criticism because of the political consequences it was feared it would have for Christians in the Middle East. A revised text on divine revelation was also discussed as was a schema on the lay apostolate. Early in October the revised schema on ecumenism was put to a series of votes and approved.

Opposition to the Döpfner plan and to a premature closing of the Council grew during the early weeks of the third period, and it was to show itself when the drastically reduced and so-called "minor schemas" came before the fathers. On October 12 a revised schema of 12 propositions "on the life and ministry of priests" was brought before the Council; it was attacked by many fathers as inadequate, superficial, jejune, and disappointing; by a vote of 930 to 1,199 it was sent back to the competent commission to be completely recast. The discussion of the schema on the Church's missionary activity was initiated by Paul VI himself, but despite his favorable judgment of it, most of the speakers found it unsatisfactory because of its brevity and skeletal nature, and at the proposal of the commission the fathers by a vote of 1,601 to 311 remanded it to be completely rewritten. The schema of 19 propositions on the renewal of the religious life was also criticized but was accepted by a narrow margin (1,155 to 882) provided that it be extensively modified to take account of the thousands of reservations (*modi*) expressed. The schema of 22 propositions on education for the priesthood was more favorably received and was substantially adopted. The schema on Christian education, developed from the inadequate previous schema of propositions on Catholic schools, was substantially approved in spite of 419 negative votes. A brief document (*votum*) on the sacrament of marriage, intended for the guidance of the commission for revising the Code of Canon Law was discussed, and by vote the fathers accepted the moderators' proposal to submit the schema to the pope for his action in accord with their two-day discussion.

The Council also discussed the schema on the Oriental Catholic Churches and the long-awaited schema of a constitution on the Church in the world of today, commonly called Schema 13 from the number of its place on the agenda. The debate on the latter focused on the methodology of the schema, on whether it properly distinguished and related the realms of the natural and the supernatural, and on the appropriateness of a council addressing the very contingent questions discussed in appendices to the schema. The fathers were admonished to avoid the subject of artificial contraception, which the pope had reserved to the study of a special group of clerical and lay experts and to his own final judgment.

Four events in the last days of the third period were received so poorly by substantial numbers of the fathers that they spoke of "the black week." Because a minority persisted in its objections to the third chapter of the schema on the Church, the pope ordered that an "explanatory note" be prefaced to the Doctrinal Commission's explanation of the final revisions; drawn up to allay the minority's fears, this text was declared to provide the authoritative interpretation of the doctrine contained in the third chapter. Although the Council was never given an opportunity to discuss or to approve this note, it succeeded in its purpose and in a vote on November 17 only 47 out of 2,146 fathers were opposed to the text.

On November 20, the revised text on the Church's relationship with non-Christian religions was approved by the Council with the provision that recommended amendments would be taken into account. The revised schema on religious freedom suffered a different fate. It was distributed to the fathers on November 17 and, according to the moderators' decision was to be voted on two days later. Since the new schema differed considerably in structure, length, and argument from the text discussed earlier in the period, some fathers requested more time for study and consultation; to accommodate them, the moderators and presidents decided to take a preliminary vote to determine whether or not the fathers wished to proceed at once to the scheduled vote. But on the appointed day (November 19) Cardinal Tisserant in the name of the presidents announced that no vote would be taken in that period. Amid strong feelings of disappointment and resentment an urgent petition for an immediate vote, drawn up by U.S. bishops, was circulated in the council hall and was signed by 441 fathers (and later by hundreds more); it was then presented to Paul VI by Cardinals Albert Meyer (Chicago), Joseph Ritter (Saint Louis), and Paul Leger (Montreal). The Pope upheld the decision to postpone the vote on the grounds that the *Ordo* required more time, but he promised that the schema on religious freedom would be the first item on the agenda of the fourth period.

On the same day, November 19, 19 modifications, which at the last minute had been introduced by papal mandate into the schema on ecumenism by the Secretariat for Christian Unity were distributed to the fathers; they were accepted by them the next day in the final vote on the whole schema, the alternative being rejection of the whole schema. The modifications were intended to clarify the text, but many of them were found offensive to and by Protestants.

At the public session that ended the third period, Paul VI concelebrated Mass with 24 priests having major Marian shrines in their territories. Then the fathers passed the constitution on the Church (2,151 to 5), the decree on the Oriental Catholic Churches (2,110 to 39), and the decree on ecumenism (2,137 to 11), and the pope promulgated them. In his closing address the Pope, having expressed his pleasure at the doctrine concerning the episcopate and the Church in general, proclaimed on his own authority Mary to be the "Mother of the Church," that is, of all the faithful and all the pastors. The Council had followed the Doctrinal Commission's advice and declined to accord her this title explicitly and had contented itself with presenting the idea in equivalent terms. Many saw the pope's act as intended to reassert his own distinct papal authority.

D. Fourth Period. Paul VI opened the fourth and last period of the Council at a public session on September 14, 1965, at which he again concelebrated Mass with 24 fathers.

He announced that he was establishing (by the *motu proprio Apostolica Sollicitudo*, dated September 15) a Synod of Bishops previously promised and as the fathers were requesting in the as yet unfinished schema on the pastoral office of bishops; in this way the close cooperation between the pope and the bishops could continue to benefit the Church even after the end of the Council.

Of the 16 final documents of Vatican II, 11 were completed, approved, and promulgated at public sessions during the fourth period; 5 texts were promulgated on October 15, 2 on November 18, and 4 on December 7. The pace of developments was rapid, and to expedite matters opportunities for the bishops to intervene orally in the hall were reduced even more than during the third period.

As the pope had promised, the schema on religious freedom was the first discussed, and while opposition to it continued to be voiced, a preliminary vote on it taken on September 21 found that a majority of 1,997 to 224 had accepted it as the basis for a definitive text. This overwhelming success represented one of the high-points for the U.S. bishops and for their chief adviser on the issue, John Courtney Murray, SJ. Amended further, and with some last-minute changes from the pope, it was approved on October 15 by vote of 1,954 to 249.

The schema on the Church in the modern world had been greatly expanded by the inclusion of the appendices to the previous draft. Differences among progressives appeared with regard to this text with some fathers, particularly Germans, arguing that it was too positive, neglecting realities of sin, and confused the realms of the natural and the supernatural. The French-speaking bishops and theologians defended its incarnational approach. A rather evangelical approach, articulated by Cardinal Lercaro, was particularly upset that the text was not stronger in its section on war and peace. This section was criticized also, but on nearly opposite grounds, by some U.S. bishops on the grounds that it ignored the deterrent role played by nuclear weapons and implied criticism of the defense policies of the west. Some controversy also arose over the sections on marriage and the relationship among its ends and on the regulation of births. A large number of bishops were also upset that their plea for an explicit condemnation of communism was not seriously considered. On December 6 the schema was approved by a vote of 2,111 to 251.

The revised schema on divine revelation continued to be the subject of debate, particularly on the question of the relationship between scripture and tradition, on inerrancy, and on the historical character of the Gospels. Last-minute interventions of the pope once again reduced opposition, and the text was approved on October 29 by a vote of 2,081 to 27.

All the other texts went through the final stages of their redaction and approval without great controversy; the schemas were the pastoral office of bishops, renewal of religious life, priestly formation, Christian education, the Church's relation to non-Christian religions, the apostolate of the laity, the Church's missionary activity, and the ministry and life of priests.

In a dramatic event on December 7, the day before the Council closed, Paul VI and Patriarch Athenagoras I, in order to remove the psychological barrier to reconciliation, expressed their regret for the mutual excommunications of the Roman See and Patriarchate of Constantinople in 1054 and for the offensive words, unfounded reproaches, and reprehensible gestures that accompanied those acts on both sides. They also expressed a desire to remove the memory of those events from the midst of the Church and committed them to oblivion. Finally, they deplored the preceding and subsequent untoward incidents, which, under the influence of various factors including lack of mutual understanding and trust, ultimately led to the effective rupture of ecclesiastical communion.

The last public session of the Council was held outdoors in front of Saint Peter's Basilica on December 8, 1965. After a Mass celebrated by the pope alone, a series of messages to the world, composed in French, were read out: to rulers, scholars, artists, women, workers, the poor and sick, and youth [see separate chapter]. The apostolic brief *In Spiritu Sancto* ordering the closure of the Council was then read by the secretary general [see separate chapter] and the acclamations traditional at ecumenical councils since the fifth century were chanted, and the fathers professed their obedience to the conciliar decrees.

To acquaint the faithful with the teachings of the Council and to stimulate them to acceptance of its decrees, to incite them to the desired spiritual renewal in their private, domestic, public, and social life and to gratitude to God for the Council, and to develop in them a feeling for and an awareness of the Church, Paul VI, by the apostolic constitution, *Mirificus Eventus* (December 7, 1965), proclaimed an extraordinary jubilee to be celebrated in all the dioceses of the world from January 1 to May 29 (Pentecost), 1966. By the *motu proprio Integrae Servandae* (December 7, 1965) he changed the name of the Holy Office to the Congregation for the Doctrine of the Faith and altered its procedure. Then, by the *motu proprio Finis Concilii* (January 11, 1966) he established post-conciliar commissions for (1) bishops and the governance of dioceses, (2) religious, (3) the missions, (4) Christian education, and (5) the apostolate of the laity, all of which were composed of the same chairmen, members and secretaries as the corresponding conciliar commissions had been, and were to be assisted by experts chosen especially from among the conciliar *periti*. He established also a new central commission for the purpose of supervising the work of the other five commissions and of interpreting the documents of the Council. Finally, he confirmed the permanent existence of the three secretariats: for promoting Christian Unity, for Non-Christian Religions, and for Non-Believers.

IV. Pronouncements of the Council. The Council issued a total of sixteen documents: four constitutions, nine decrees, and three declarations.

A.   Constitutions. These four documents covered the Church, divine revelation, liturgy, and the Church in the modern world.

1. Dogmatic Constitution on the Church (Lumen Gentium). In the fathers' discussion of this constitution the principal points centered on: Biblical figures for the Church; the Church as a Mystery; the theological, spiritual, and juridical aspects of the Church; the relation between Christ's Church and the Roman Catholic Church; the position of separated Christians and of non-Christians vis-à-vis the Church; the authority of the body of bishops (collegiality) and its relations to the papal primacy; restoration of the permanent diaconate with or without celibacy; universal priesthood of the faithful; functions of the laity and their relation to the hierarchy; existence and role of charisms; the position of separated Christians and of non-Christians vis-à-vis the Church; balance between equality and authority; concern for the poor and the afflicted and for social justice; the missionary obligation of the Church; relations between Church and State; and the Blessed Virgin Mary as mediatrix of grace and as mother of the Church.

The constitution has the following chapters: (1) "The Mystery of the Church," (2) "The People of God," (3) "The Hierarchical Structure of the Church and the Episcopate in Particular," (4) "The Laity," (5) "The Universal Call to Holiness in the Church,"

(6) "Religious," (7) "The Eschatological Nature of the Pilgrim Church and its Union with the Church in Heaven," and (8) "The Blessed Virgin Mary, Mother of God, in the Mystery of Christ and of the Church."

2. *Dogmatic Constitution on Divine Revelation (Dei Verbum).* The discussion centered on the nature of tradition and its relation to Scripture; whether all revelation in somehow contained in the Scriptures; inerrancy of the Bible, historicity of the Gospels; and reading, diffusion, and interpretation of the Bible. The chapters of the constitution are: (1) "Revelation Itself," (2) "The Handing on of Divine Revelation," (3) "Sacred Scripture," (4) "The Old Testament," (5) "The New Testament," and (6) "Sacred Scripture in the Life of the Church."

3. *Constitution on the Sacred Liturgy (Sacrosanctum Concilium).* The conciliar discussion touched on the Biblical, Christological, and ecclesiological foundations of the liturgy; its didactic value; liturgy as a unifying factor; the best ways to secure active and intelligent participation; simplification of rites; use of Latin and of modern languages; incorporation of local or national customs or traditions; making liturgy an effective influence in society; the competence of episcopal conferences and of individual bishops; concelebration of Mass; Communion under both kinds; Anointing of the Sick; and the length, language, and composition of the Breviary.

In addition to an introduction, which states that the liturgy is the outstanding means whereby the faithful express in their lives and manifest to others the mystery of Christ and the real nature of the true Church, the constitution contains the following chapters: (1) "General Principles for the Restoration and Promotion of the Sacred Liturgy," (2) "The Most Sacred Mystery of the Eucharist," (3) "The Other Sacraments and the

Sacramentals," (4) "The Divine Office," (5) "The Liturgical Year," (6) "Sacred Music," and (7) "Sacred Art and Sacred Furnishings." An appendix contains "A Declaration on the Revision of the Calendar."

4. Pastoral Constitution on the Church in the Modern World (Gaudium et Spes). The fathers discussed the meaning and value of temporal activity; dignity of the human person; the conflict in the world between good and evil; the presence of sin; the role of women in society; racial discrimination; problems of the third world; world poverty and hunger; problems of emigration; atheism, Marxism, and communism; freedom and encouragement of scholarly research; the Church's influence on culture; Christian humanism and anthropology; the equality of all human beings; the necessity for Catholics to work with all people of good will; the solidarity of the Church with the world; the light shed by revelation on the mentality, problems, and forces of our age; the benefits of religion to civilization; the nature, ends, acts, and indissolubility of marriage; family life; abortion; economic production; the conditions of workers; relations between the Church and political society; the arms race; the possession and use of nuclear weapons; obligatory military service and conscientious objection; the obligations of nations toward an international authority; the growth of world population; aid to underdeveloped nations.

The constitution contains an introductory statement on "The Situation of People in the Contemporary World." Part I, entitled "The Church and the Human Person's Calling," consists of four chapters: "The Dignity of the Human Person," "The Community of Mankind," "Human Activity throughout the World," and "The Role of the Church in the Modern World." Part II, entitled "Some Problems of Special Urgency," has five chapters: "Marriage and the Family," "Development of Culture," "Economic and Social Life," "Political Community," and "Peace and the Community of

Nations." A concluding section states that the Church desires honest dialogue between her own members, with the separated brethren and communities, with all who acknowledge God, with those who cultivate the noble qualities of the human spirit without believing in God, and even with those who oppress the Church.

B. Decrees. The Council issued nine decrees on a wide range of topics.

1. Decree on the Pastoral Office of Bishops (Christus Dominus). The discussions centered on the bishop's office and the powers needed to exercise it; the Roman Curia and its relations with bishops; internationalization of the Curia; the powers needed for the proper discharge of bishops' duties; freedom in the appointment of bishops; compulsory retirement of bishops; the subjection of religious to the local ordinary; care for migrants; personal dioceses for people of a peculiar rite or nationality; powers of episcopal conferences; and, a central organ of bishops to assist the pope in governing the Church.

2. Decree on Ecumenism (Unitatis Redintegratio). Points of discussion included: the need of humility, charity, forgiveness, and the acknowledgement of errors and faults of all parties; assurance that unity does not mean uniformity; no simple "return" of the separated brethren; the meaning and use of the word "ecumenism"; the propriety of calling certain Protestant communities "churches"; the danger of engendering confusion and indifferentism in the minds of the faithful; participation in religious services with non-Catholic Christians; the validity of marriages celebrated before non-Catholic ministers; ways of conducting the dialogue; the desire for the restoration of unity among all followers of Christ. In conclusion, the decree exhorts Catholics to refrain from superficiality and imprudent zeal, to be faithful to the truth received from the Apostles and Fathers of the

Church, and to act in conjunction with the separated brethren so that no obstacle be put in the ways of divine Providence and no preconceived judgments impair the future inspirations of the Holy Spirit.

3. *Decree on the Oriental Catholic Churches (Orientalium Ecclesiarum).* The discussion treated structure of the Church; the rights and prerogatives of patriarchs; the evils of forced Latinization; determination of the rite of Oriental converts to the Catholic Church; the participation of Oriental Catholics in the religious services of Oriental non-Catholics and vice versa (*communicatio in sacris*); and marriages between Oriental Catholics and non-Catholics. The decree expresses the Catholic Church's esteem for the institutions, liturgical rites, ecclesiastical traditions, and the established standards of Christian life of Oriental Catholics.

4. *Decree on the Ministry and Life of Priests (Presbyterorum Ordinis).* Central points of discussion included: the dignity and excellence of the priesthood; the spirituality and holiness of priests; the connection between their spiritual life and their ministry; their participation in Christ's priesthood; obedience and poverty; the importance of celibacy; life in common; associations of priests; their relations with bishops and laymen; an advisory council for the bishop; rights of priests; their duties toward non-Catholics; extraparochial apostolates; training in preaching; their intellectual activity and continued education in the ministry; the administration of the Sacrament of Penance; the missionary dimension of the priesthood; the equitable distribution of priests throughout the world; remuneration and financial equality of priests; abolition of the system of benefices and of honorary titles; and care for ill, aged, and fallen priests. The preface of the decree states that the decree applies to all priests.

5. *Decree on Education for the Priesthood (Optatam*

Totius). Points of discussion included: the notion of a vocation to the priesthood and means of fostering it; the nature and purpose of minor seminaries; adaptation of seminary discipline to modern times and to life in the world; organic unity in the spiritual, intellectual, and pastoral formation of candidates for the priesthood; sending them from other parts of the world to study in Europe; the place of scholasticism, especially Thomism, in the teaching of philosophy and theology; the need of natural, human virtues in candidates; the development of a missionary or apostolic spirit in them; isolation of seminarians from the world; a period for acquiring preliminary experience in the ministry or else a pastoral apprenticeship after ordination; and, reform of the Congregation of Seminaries.

6. *Decree on the Renewal of Religious Life (Perfectae Caritatis).* Renewal according to the Gospel was discussed, as well as the attitude toward traditional practices; the theology of the vows; the role of contemplatives; the place of the apostolate in religious life; accommodation to contemporary needs; the spirituality of the active life; the recent decrease of vocations; and, conferences of major superiors. The decree asserts that the adapted renewal includes both the constant return to the sources of all Christian life and to the original spirit of the institutes and their adaptation to changed conditions and the needs of the Church. The religious life is a state complete in itself and should be held in high esteem. The vows of chastity, poverty and obedience are related to dedication to the love and service of God and to the works of the apostolate. Priests and religious educators should foster religious vocations.

7. *Decree on the Missionary Activity of the Church (Ad Gentes).* Conciliar discussion covered: the theology of the missions; the nature of the missionary vocation; flexibility and adaptation to other cultures with their own customs

and values; creation of a central mission board; the new role of the Congregation for the Propagation of the Faith; the reason for missionary activity; the need of it for the salvation of non-Christians; dialogue with non-Christians; connection of missionary activity with ecumenism; extension of the mission area to other territories; the situation of the "new churches"; the status of prelatures *nullius;* the relations between missionary institutes and local ecclesiastical jurisdictions; the apostolic training of missionaries and catechists; borrowing of priests; lay missionaries; support of the missions; and, twinning or pairing of an older diocese with a new jurisdiction.

8. Decree on the Apostolate of the Laity (Apostolicam Actuositatem).   Points discussed included: the dogmatic foundation of this apostolate and its objectives; lay spirituality; formation for the apostolate; relations with the hierarchy; Catholic Action; lay initiative and clericalism; the apostolate of youth; social action; cooperation with non-Catholics and non-Christians; and, a secretariat in the Roman Curia.

9. Decree on the Media of Social Communication (Inter Mirifica).   The responsibility of the laity in this area was discussed, as well as the use of the media for evangelization; the need of concrete assistance in personnel and equipment in missionary countries; the formation of sound public opinion; institution of a special office in the Roman Curia or expansion of the then existing Pontifical Commission; and, creation of an international Catholic news agency. The Council asks the pope to extend the duties and competence of the Secretariat for the Supervision of Publications and Entertainment to embrace all media, including the press, and to appoint to it experts from various countries, including laymen.

C. Declarations. The Council issued three declarations.

1. Declaration on Religious Freedom (Dignitatis Humanae). Points of discussion included: philosophical and juridical and/or dogmatic and theological arguments; connection between internal, personal freedom and external, social freedom; limitations; development of the Church's earlier teaching, especially of the doctrine of previous popes; effects on Catholic countries and on concordats; "rights of error"; danger of giving an excuse to antireligious governments; freedom or toleration; right of evangelization or of proselytism; danger of promoting indifferentism; rights of the Catholic Church; and, application to predominantly non-Catholic countries and to those under Communist domination.

Part I of the declaration, "The General Principles of Religious Freedom," states that the human person has a right to immunity from coercion on the part of individuals, social groups, or any human power. Government should respect and favor the religious life of the citizenry but should not command or inhibit religious acts; in preventing abuses, it must act according to juridical norms for the preservation of public order. Part II, "Religious Freedom in the Light of Revelation," asserts that the human person's response to God in faith must be free. The Church must enjoy freedom and independence. The Council denounces and deplores the oppressive policies of some governments and emphasizes the necessity of religious freedom, which should everywhere be provided with an effective constitutional guarantee.

2. Declaration on the Church's Attitude toward Non-Christian Religions (Nostra Aetate). The discussion covered: religious, not political, motives for a pronouncement in view of Arab opposition; the common religious patrimony of Christians and Jews; the alleged collective guilt of the Jewish people for the death of Christ (the accusation of deicide); their alleged rejection by God; the prediction of their eventual conversion to Christianity; the urgency of condemning anti-Semitism; and, bonds with Islam and other world religions. The declaration affirms that all peoples have one community, origin, and goal. People ask fundamental religious questions. The Church deplores hatred and persecution of the Jews and all displays of anti-Semitism and reproves any discrimination or harassment based on race, color, social status, or religion.

3.   *Declaration on Christian Education (Gravissimum Educationis).* The discussion covered: objectives; role of the family; obligations and limitations of the state; parents' right freely to choose schools; freedom within Catholic schools and freedom of research, especially in the sacred sciences; duties of the postconciliar commission. The declaration recognizes the importance of education for young people and adults amid present-day progress. All persons have a right to education; children have a right to moral instruction. The Church is obliged to educate its children, and it uses all suitable aids, such as catechetical instruction, but especially schools. In Catholic colleges and universities individual disciplines should be pursued according to their own principles and methods and with freedom of research, and there should be, if not a faculty, at least an institute or chair of theology with courses for lay students.   [NOTE: This presentation has been edited by J. Kroeger; it is taken from *New Catholic Encyclopedia, Second Edition* (2003) XIV: 407-418; reprint permission through FABC.]

3

VATICAN II REFORM
The Basic Principles

Avery Dulles, S.J.

On January 25, 1985, Pope John Paul II unexpectedly called an extraordinary session of the synod of bishops to meet from November 25 to December 8, 1985. This meeting, commemorating the twentieth anniversary of the conclusion of Vatican II, was to give the bishops from the various national and regional conferences an opportunity to exchange and deepen the experience of applying the Council to the life of the Church. To allay any fears that he might be distancing himself from Vatican II, the pope declared that it "remains the fundamental event in the life of the contemporary Church," and that for himself personally it has been "the constant reference point of every pastoral action."

In the past two decades (1965-1985) Vatican II has become, for many Catholics, a center of controversy. A few voices from the extreme right and the extreme left frankly reject the Council. Reactionaries of the traditionalist variety censure it for having yielded to Protestant and Modernist tendencies. Radicals of the far left, conversely, complain that the Council, while making some progress, failed to do away with the Church's absolutistic claims and its antiquated class structures. The vast majority of Catholics, expressing satisfaction with the results of the Council, are still divided because they interpret the Council in contrary ways. The conservatives, insisting on continuity with the past, give primary emphasis to the Council's reaffirmation of settled Catholic doctrines, including papal primacy and infallibility. The progressives, however, hold that the true meaning of the Council is to be found rather in its innovations. For them Vatican II made a decisive break with the juridicism, clericalism, and triumphalism of recent centuries and laid the foundations for a more liberal and healthier Catholicism.

Like most other Councils, Vatican II issued a number of compromise statements. It intentionally spoke ambiguously on certain points, leaving to the future the achievement of greater clarity.   Many commentators, accenting these problematical features, give the impression that the Council left nothing but doubt and confusion in its wake. It may therefore be time to acknowledge that, while leaving many open questions, the Council did present a solid core of unequivocal teaching on matters of great importance.

Vatican II addressed an extraordinary variety of issues, ranging from highly technical questions about the theology of revelation to eminently practical questions about marriage and family life. But its central focus was undoubtedly the self-understanding of the Church, and this is the theme that the present pope evidently envisages as the agenda for the 1985 synod. As a contribution to the common reflection that precedes the synod, I shall here attempt to set forth, as simply as I can, the basic vision of the Church as understood by Vatican II. I shall concentrate on practical and pastoral matters that have a direct impact on the lives of rank-and-file Catholics. For the sake of clarity, I shall arrange my observations under the rubric of ten principles which I regard as unquestionably endorsed by the Council. Whoever does not accept all ten of these principles, I would contend, cannot honestly claim to have accepted the results of Vatican II.

1. *Aggiornamento.* This Italian term, which may be translated by English words such as "updating," "modernization," or "adaptation," was popularized by John XXIII, who made the concept fundamental to his own program for the coming Council. Accepting this program, the fathers at Vatican II abjured the hostility and suspicion toward the modern world that had characterized the Catholicism of the nineteenth and early twentieth centuries. Especially in the *Pastoral Constitution on the Church in the Modern World (Gaudium et Spes),* the Council declared its great respect for the truth and goodness that have been brought into the world through modernization (GS 42). It stated that we are witnesses to the birth of a new humanism in which people are conscious of their responsibility to one another for the future of the world (GS 55). The faithful, said the Council, must "live in very close union with the men of their time" (GS 62). Catholics must, moreover, "blend modern science and its theories and the understanding of the most recent discoveries with Christian morality and doctrine" (GS 62), so that the Church may keep pace with the times and enter fully into the new age now being born. In so doing the Church can enrich itself and better understand the treasures she has received from Christ. Far from clinging to ancient forms, the Church as pilgrim must press forward toward the consummation of history, when God's kingdom will be revealed in its fullness. Neither John XXIII nor the Council, of course, held the absurd dogma that the new is always better than the old. In fact, they frequently pointed out that modern techniques can easily be abused so as to distract people from the lasting goods of the spirit. But that is no excuse for burying oneself in the past.

The principle of *aggiornamento*, like all the others we shall consider, is only a principle. To apply it requires prudence and discretion lest the Gospel, in being accommodated to the spirit of the age, lose its challenging power. Still the principle itself is sound and important. The Church, glorying in its magnificent heritage, should not allow itself to become a museum piece. It must not become a relic of the Middle Ages or any past period, but rather a vital part of the modern world as it presses forward into God's future. Confident that the Lord himself remains with his people down through the centuries, Christians can have the courage to live out the Gospel and bear witness to it under the conditions of today's world.

2. The Reformability of the Church. In recent centuries it has been common to look upon the Church as a divine institution without spot or wrinkle. While admitting the faults of individual believers, Catholics have insisted that the Church itself is pure and holy. Vatican II, however, depicted the Church in terms of the biblical image of the People of God. As we learn from Scripture, this people, though always sealed by its covenant relationship with God, was sometimes unfaithful. *The Constitution on the Church (Lumen Gentium)*, therefore, was able to admit: "The Church, embracing sinners in her bosom, is at the same time holy and always in need of being purified, and incessantly pursues the path of penance and renewal" (LG 8). Furthermore, in the *Decree on Ecumenism (Unitatis Redintegratio)*, the Council declared: "Christ summons the Church, as she goes her pilgrim way, to that continual reformation of which she always has need, insofar as she is an institution of human beings here on earth" (UR 6).

The idea that the Church might be reformable caught many Catholics by surprise. In the late Middle Ages there had been several Councils having as their express aim the reformation of the whole Church "in the head and in the members," but after the Protestant Reformation the idea of reform came under suspicion in Catholic circles. Thanks to Vatican II, however, we are relieved of the burden of having to defend the whole record of the past. We can freely admit that not only individual Catholics, but the Church itself in its official actions, has committed errors and sins, such as the burning of heretics, the persecutions of Jews, and the excesses of holy wars. We can admit that Catholics had a large share of responsibility in bringing on the divisions among Christians that so weaken the Christian witness in our time.

Like the principle of updating, this second principle must be applied with discretion. Not everything in the Church is suspect and fallible. Its basic sacramental structures, its scriptures, and its dogmas are abidingly valid. The grace of Christ, which comes through these channels, is more powerful than human infidelity and sin. The Church, therefore, does not have an equal affinity to holiness and to evil. Evil is against its true nature. For this reason Vatican II, while speaking of the Church of sinners, avoided the expression "sinful Church." The difference is a subtle one, but has a certain importance.

With regard to past historical events, we should be on guard against a kind of spiritual masochism that would transfer all the blame from the other party to our own. Often it is best to follow the principle of John XXIII: "We do not wish to conduct a trial of the past. We shall not seek to establish who was right and who was wrong. Responsibility is divided." Still, to set the record straight, it is well to disavow certain errors. An example would be the present investigation to determine whether the papal commission erred by condemning the theories of Galileo in the seventeenth century.

3. Renewed Attention to the Word of God. In the Middle Ages and even more since the Reformation, Catholicism tended to become the Church of law and the sacraments rather than the Church of the Gospel and the Word. Catholics too often neglected the spiritual riches contained in the Bible. Emphasizing the precepts of the Church, they allowed the proclamation of the good news to fall into abeyance. They celebrated the

Mass in Latin—a language not understood by most of the people—and usually without any homily. In Catholic theology the Bible was viewed as a remote source of doctrine, hardly used except to find proof texts for later Church doctrines.

Vatican II, especially in its *Constitution on Divine Revelation (Dei Verbum),* recovered the primacy of Scripture as the Word of God consigned to writing under the inspiration of the Holy Spirit (DV 9). The teaching office of the Church, according to the constitution, "is not above the word of God but serves it, listening to it devoutly, guarding it scrupulously, and explaining it faithfully..." (DV 10). "The study of the sacred page," according to the same constitution, "is, so to speak, the soul of sacred theology" (DV 24).

The same constitution strongly recommended the use of Scripture by all Catholics. "Easy access to sacred Scripture," it stated, "should be provided for all the Christian faithful" (DV 22). The Scriptures were here compared to the Eucharist, since each in its own way offers to the faithful the bread of life (DV 21). And in the same paragraph we find the following eloquent sentence: "For in the sacred books, the Father who is in heaven meets His children with great love and speaks with them; and the force and power of the Word of God is so great that it remains the support and energy of the Church, the strength of faith for her children, the food of the soul, the pure and perennial source of spiritual life."

Besides rehabilitating the Bible, the Council sought to renew the ministry of preaching. It called on Catholic preachers to provide the nourishment of the Scriptures to the People of God (DV 23) and warned that, as Augustine had said, "those who do not listen to the Word of God inwardly will be empty preachers of the Word of God outwardly" (DV 25). Thus, priests as well as lay people were exhorted to read the Scriptures prayerfully.

Since the Council, directives such as those I have just quoted have produced excellent fruits. Catholics have learned more about the Bible; many of them attend study and prayer groups that concentrate on the Scriptures. But in this respect, as in others, further progress remains necessary. There is as yet no danger that Catholics, in their enthusiasm for the Word, will turn away from ritual and sacrament or that, in their devotion to the Gospel, they will neglect the law of Christ and the Church. The more relaxed attitude toward Church law at the present time, while regrettable in some respects, can be viewed as a gain insofar as it helps to overcome an almost pharisaical scrupulosity to which Catholics were subject in the years before Vatican II. Ideally, of course, contrasting elements such as law and gospel, word and sacrament, should not be played off against each other but should rather be mutually reinforcing. The effort to achieve the right balance should be high on the agenda of Catholics today.

4. Collegiality. It is almost a platitude to assert that the Catholic Church, from the Middle Ages until Vatican II, was pyramidal in structure. Truth and holiness were conceived as emanating from the pope as commander-in-chief at the top, and the bishops were depicted as subordinate officers carrying out the orders of the pope. In our day many conservative Catholics lean toward this military analogy of the Church.

Vatican II did not deny the primacy of the pope as it had been defined a century earlier by Vatican I, but it did put the papacy into a significantly new context. The college of bishops, together with the pope as its head, was seen as having the fullness of power in the Church. The individual bishops were portrayed not as mere lieutenants of the pope but as pastors in their own right. They were in fact called "vicars of Christ" (LG 28) an ancient title that had been given to bishops in the early

Church but which, since about the eighth century, had come to be reserved to the pope.

The principle of collegiality runs through the documents of Vatican II like a golden thread. Just as the pope is surrounded by a college of bishops, so each bishop serves as head of a presbyteral college, called presbytery, and governs his diocese in consultation with presbyters, religious, and laity. Thus, the principle of collegiality, understood in a wide sense, may be viewed as pervading all levels of the Church. Pastors, according to the *Constitution on the Church*, "know that they themselves were not meant by Christ to shoulder alone the entire saving mission of the Church toward the world. On the contrary, they understand that it is their noble duty so to shepherd the faithful and recognize their services and charismatic gifts that all according to their proper roles may cooperate in this common undertaking with one heart" (LG 30).

Since the Council, many new institutions have been erected to implement collegiality on various levels; for example, the worldwide synod of bishops, national and regional episcopal conferences, national and diocesan pastoral Councils, parish Councils, priests' senates, and the like. If in some cases too many questions have been subjected to prolonged discussion and debate, it has been necessary to go through this stage to arrive at the proper mean. Parliamentarianism or democracy, if carried too far, is likely to provoke a reaction in the opposite direction, toward a revival of the preconciliar form of authoritarianism, which seemed relatively efficient and rapid. Here the Council still calls upon us to devise mechanisms of decision making that respect both the traditional principle of personal pastoral authority and the nature of the Church as a Spirit-filled community. Neither an army nor a New England town meeting is a suitable paradigm.

5. Religious Freedom. Up to the very time when the Council opened, it was far from certain whether the Catholic Church could subscribe to the principle of religious freedom which had by then prevailed in most Protestant bodies and won approval in the Assembly of the World Council of Churches at New Delhi in 1961. More specifically, it was being asked whether the Church could fully respect the right and duty of each person to follow his or her conscience with regard to the acceptance or nonacceptance of religious belief. For centuries the Churches, Protestant as well as Catholic, had striven to gain control of the apparatus of civil power so as to obtain a privileged status. In the 1950s, when John Courtney Murray began to defend the idea of a religiously neutral state, his orthodoxy was questioned by other American theologians and even by some Roman authorities. Over the protests of his opponents, however, he was invited to Vatican II (not indeed to the first session but from the second session on) and he, probably more than any other individual, was responsible for the *Declaration on Religious Freedom.* This Declaration clearly taught that there is no need for the state to profess the true religion or give it a legally privileged status. It approved of civil tolerance for all faiths and rejected, on theological grounds, any coercion in the sphere of belief.

For most Americans the principle of religious freedom offers no difficulties. We almost take it for granted. Our danger is rather to fall into the opposite extreme, religious indifferentism. We have to remind ourselves that the Declaration itself asserted the unique status of the Catholic faith and the obligation of all believers to profess and defend that faith. Those who sincerely believe and love the truth received from Christ will strive, as did Christ and the apostles, to bear witness to it by their words and deeds, and to share their faith with others.

6. The Active Role of the Laity. In the Catholic Church, at least in modern times, priests and religious have borne almost total responsibility for the mission of the Church. The apostolic spirit of the clergy and religious orders has been admirable, but generally speaking, the laity has been rather passive. Seeking to remedy this situation, the movement known as Catholic Action, in the period between the two world wars, sought to involve elite members of the laity in the apostolate of the hierarchy. Not satisfied with this, some progressive theologians during the decade before Vatican II held that the laity, besides associating themselves with the apostolate of the hierarchy, should exercise an active apostolate in their own right as baptized believers. The Council, endorsing this development, exhorted lay persons to advance the kingdom of God by engaging in temporal affairs and by discharging their familial and vocational obligations in a manner faithful to Christ.

Since the Council, some have maintained that the clergy have as their proper sphere of operation the inner affairs of the Church, whereas lay persons should regard secular matters as their area of competence. The Council, however, does not authorize such a sharp division of labor. It provides for active participation of the laity in divine worship, in pastoral councils, and even in the sphere of theology. In this last area Vatican II calls upon the laity to speak freely and openly. "In order that such persons may fulfill their proper function," says *Gaudium et Spes*, "let it be recognized that all the faithful, clerical and lay, possess a lawful freedom of inquiry and of thought, and the freedom to express their minds humbly and courageously about those matters in which they enjoy competence" (GS 62).

In the two decades since the Council, we have seen in the Church a great increase of lay ministries—not only the canonically erected ministries of reader and acolyte, but also ministries of teaching, music, social action, counselling, and even the distribution of the Eucharist. There has likewise been a great and welcome influx of laymen and laywomen into theology. These new developments, predictably, have called for adjustments that have in some cases been difficult. It is the task of the pope and the bishops to see that these new developments do not disrupt the community. In some cases this means proceeding slowly, but on the whole we must be thankful that so much has been accomplished in so short a time. In a period of diminishing vocations to the clerical and religious life, it is urgent that lay persons assume greater responsibility than ever for the faith and life of the Church.

7. Regional and Local Variety. From the late Middle Ages until Vatican II the characteristic emphasis of Catholicism had been on the universal Church, commonly depicted as an almost monolithic society. Vatican II, by contrast, emphasized the local Churches, each of them under the direction of a bishop who is called, as already mentioned, a "vicar of Christ." Many of the Council texts portray the universal Church as a communion, or collegial union, of particular Churches. "In and from such individual Churches," says the Constitution on the Church, "there comes into being the one and only Catholic Church" (LG 23). The local bishop, on the ground of his ordination and appointment, is given authority to be a true pastor of his own community, making responsible decisions rather than simply carrying out Roman directives (LG 27).

Vatican II made provision also for regional groupings. Speaking of the differences between Eastern and Western Christianity, the Council declares: "Far from being an obstacle to the Church's unity, such diversity of customs and observances only adds to her comeliness, and contributes greatly to carrying out her mission" (UR 16). Vatican II accordingly recognizes a legitimate variety among regional Churches, even in the formulation of doctrine. Elsewhere it states: "The variety of local Churches with one common aspiration is particularly splendid evidence of the catholicity of the undivided Church" (LG 23). "The accommodated preaching of the Gospel," says the *Pastoral Constitution (Gaudium et Spes)* "ought to remain the law of all evangelization" (GS 44). Each nation, we are told, must develop the ability to express Christ's message in its own way, and must foster a living exchange between the Church and the particular culture (GS 44).

The differences between the Catholicism of different regions are much more evident today than twenty years ago [1965], when the customs and liturgy of the Roman Church, with its Latin language, were universally enforced. This diversification has not yet run its course. John Paul II, in a visit to Zaire, spoke in favor of Africanization.

Americanization ["Asianization"] has been and is taking place in our own Catholicism. Because of our distinctive cultural and political tradition, we have different views from most other nations [continents] on how the Church ought to relate to politics and economics. We have different conceptions regarding human rights, growing out of our common-law tradition. Probably, too, we are more prepared than many other countries to see women rise to positions of leadership in the Church, as they have in political and economic life.

While seeking a sound inculturation, we must avoid thinking that our own national traditions are above criticism, or that Americans [any nationality] are a superior people who have nothing to learn from other countries. Even where legitimate differences exist, we must take care that they do not disrupt our communion with the rest of the Catholic Church. In this regard we should respect the authority of the Holy See, which has the responsibility before God both to "protect legitimate differences" and to make sure that "such differences do not hinder unity but rather contribute to it" (LG 13).

8. Ecumenism. Since the Reformation, Catholics have commonly adopted hostile and defensive attitudes toward other Christian Churches, and especially toward Protestantism. Such hostility may even be found in official documents of the Holy See, notably between Pius IX and Pius XI. In this regard John XXIII and Vatican II effected a quiet revolution. The Council in its *Decree on Ecumenism* expressed reverence for the heritage of other Christian Churches, called attention to their salvific importance for their own members, and acknowledged that they possess true elements of the Church of Christ. As a result, *anathema* has yielded to dialogue. In the ecumenical dialogues since the Council, great progress has been achieved in overcoming major differences that have divided the Churches for centuries. While formal reunion between the Catholic Church and other communions remains only a distant prospect, Christians of different confessional groups have achieved a far greater measure of mutual understanding, respect, and solidarity.

The proper implementation of ecumenism, as of the other principles we are here considering, requires realism and good judgment. On the one hand, we must overcome our habitual attitudes of hatred and suspicion and be open to appreciate all the sound values in other forms of Christianity, both Eastern and Western. On the other hand, we cannot surrender what is true and valid in our Catholic tradition or act as though all the ecumenical problems had already been solved. Instead of simply wishing away the remaining disagreements, we must work patiently over a long period to achieve, through prayer and dialogue, a consensus based on the truth.

9. Dialogue with Other Religions. The Second Vatican

Council was not slow in perceiving that the changed attitude of Catholics toward other Christian Churches called for a corresponding shift in their attitude toward other religions and their adherents. The Council accordingly drew up a *Declaration on Non-Christian Religions (Nostra Aetate)*, which contained a major section on Jewish-Christian relationships. Since the Council, there have been important dialogues between Catholics and Jews, both in this country and abroad. Christians are finding that the riches of other religious traditions, such as Hinduism, Buddhism, and Islam, can help to revitalize their own faith and worship. Missionaries are finding new ways of helping non-Christians to relate better to God within the faiths of their ancestors.

The principle of interreligious dialogue, like the other principles I have mentioned, challenges us to a mature and responsible reaction. Some commentators have introduced an antithesis between mission and dialogue, as if the importance of the one must undercut the necessity of the other. The Council, however, kept mission and dialogue in balance. While recognizing elements of truth and goodness in all the great religions, and hence the desirability of respectful dialogue, the Council insisted on the God-given uniqueness of the Church of Christ and consequently on the "absolute necessity" of missionary activity so that Christ may be acknowledged among all peoples as universal Lord and Savior.

For most Christians the most obvious application of the *Declaration on Non-Christian Religions* has to do with Judaism; there is still among many Catholics a latent attitude of hostility, deeply rooted in ethnic and cultural factors. We need to make a special effort to rise above these negative attitudes, which are utterly contrary to the gospel precept of love. As I mentioned earlier, the Church collectively has much to repent of in its historic dealings with the Jewish people. Let us not add to these crimes.

10. The Social Mission of the Church. Since the Reformation the Catholic Church has tended to regard its mission as an exclusively religious one, aimed at preparing individuals through faith, worship, and right behavior to attain eternal life. Gradually, with the social encyclicals of popes such as Leo XIII and Pius XI, the Church began to assume responsibility to teach the principles of a just social order, but this order was viewed in terms of conformity to the natural law rather than as an implementation of the Gospel.

With John XXIII and Vatican II, the emphasis shifted. The apostolate of peace and social justice came to be seen as a requirement of the Church's mission to carry on the work of Christ, who had compassion on the poor and the oppressed. This changed attitude was eloquently expressed in Vatican II's "Message to Humanity," released nine days after the opening of the Council in 1962. It was more fully elaborated in the *Pastoral Constitution on the Church in the Modern World (Gaudium et Spes),* which described the Church as endowed with "a function, a light, and an energy which can serve to structure and consolidate the human community" (GS 42). Since the Council this trend has gained momentum. It was reflected in the encyclical of Paul VI on the *Progress of Peoples* (1967) and even more clearly in the synod document on *Justice in the World* (1971), which depicted the struggle for justice and the transformation of society as constitutive dimensions of evangelization. Seeking to carry out the Council's mandate to discern the signs of the times in the light of the Gospel (GS 4), popes and episcopal conferences have given increasingly concrete directives concerning matters of public policy. The theme of the Church's special solidarity with the poor, already broached at Vatican II (GS 1), has given rise in Latin America to the idea of a "preferential option" for the poor.

This tenth principle is no easier to implement than the other nine. It would be irresponsible for the Church to avoid all comment on the moral and religious aspects of public policy issues, for the world legitimately looks to religious leaders for advice in reshaping society, according to what Bishop James Malone has called "a God-given value system." On the other hand, ecclesiastical authorities must respect the freedom of individuals and groups within the Church to reach conscientious decisions about policies on which intelligent and committed Catholics can disagree. The turbulent debates surrounding the collective pastorals of the American bishops on peace and on the economy make it evident that, while real progress is being made, the right approach to sociopolitical issues is only gradually being found through a process of trial and error.

These ten principles are not intended to exhaust the achievements of Vatican II, even in the field of ecclesiology. But they do show, in my opinion, that the Council, in spite of all hesitations and compromises, gave clear directives on a number of crucial issues. The extraordinary synod of 1985, commemorating the twentieth anniversary of the close of the Council, may reaffirm and clarify some of these basic, unequivocal teachings. It could in this way assist Catholics all over the world to address the problems of the coming decades with greater confidence and unanimity. [NOTE: This presentation has been slightly edited by J. Kroeger; it originally was published in *Church* (Summer, 1985): 3-10; reprint permission through FABC.]

4

THE STRUGGLE OF VATICAN II
An Interview with Denis E. Hurley, O.M.I.

Archbishop Denis E. Hurley O.M.I. led the South African Catholic Church for forty-five years (1947-1992) through intense social upheaval, especially through the nation's struggle against apartheid. Hurley was also an active Church leader, involved with ICEL (International Commission on English in the Liturgy). He remembers well his experience at the Second Vatican Council in this interview which was conducted in October 2000.

QUESTION: Could you tell us a bit about your background and your early days as head of the Church in South Africa?

ANSWER: I was ordained in Rome as a member of the Oblates of Mary Immaculate in 1939. In May 1940 we were told that if we wanted to get out of Italy, we had better leave. So I returned to South Africa where I had been born in 1915. My father had been the son of a farmer in West Cork, Ireland, and to escape the farm he joined the British navy. The navy took him to South Africa during the Boer War. He left the navy and went into the lighthouse service. He served at Cape Point and then on Robben Island, where later Nelson Mandela was imprisoned. We spent three years on Robben Island. I once told Nelson Mandela that I had been on Robben Island long before he had.

I was assigned as an assistant priest in the Emmanuel Cathedral, Durban, and three years later appointed superior of a small Oblate seminary. In March 1947, I was ordained bishop of what was then called the Vicariate Apostolic of Natal. I was just thirty-one, for a year the youngest Catholic bishop in the world. It seemed as if Rome had confused my consecration with my confirmation.

The Church in South Africa was strongly white-oriented though largely black in numbers. I felt that we had to respond more fully to the situation and that there had to be much more consultation among the priests about how we were to proceed. So I spent some time in gatherings of priests. I was concerned about the injustices we could see all around us.

Q: On January 25, 1959, when Pope John XXIII announced that he was going to convene a Council, what did you think?

A: It caught me by surprise. I had been brought up to believe that Councils were called when a heresy was breaking out and you had to deal with Arians or Lutherans or some such. I did not see any great heresy afflicting the Church at the time. So I wondered why there was going to be a Council. I didn't respond very quickly to the first request for items for the agenda for Cardinal Tardini. Then he sent us a reminder, so I pulled out the Latin dictionary and grammar and wrote out some points. Quite a few of them related to the social mission of the Church, another concerned liturgy. I don't think I went as far as saying "give up the Latin."

To my surprise I was selected for the Central Preparatory

Commission. I thought it was because Rome did not have up-to-date information on the situation in South Africa and thought I was still chair of the episcopal conference, whereas Archbishop McCann (later Cardinal) had taken over. I went to Rome and right away realized that we were up against something: a big division between conservatives and progressives.

Those resident in Rome, mainly cardinals, were strongly conservative in regard to theological attitudes, the training of priests, and the preservation of the Church in the established tradition. By contrast, I found myself wholly in sympathy with the transalpine cardinals like Alfrink, Frings, König, and so on. Cardinal Suenens was not there at the beginning. The transalpines were progressives who had been taking part in the great theological resurgence in Western Europe, under the Congars, the Chenus, the Rahners. I found myself immediately in sympathy with them. I had done a good deal of reading in the late forties and through the fifties; it was an exciting decade for me. It opened up my mind and heart to a different view of theology from the Scholastic "mathematics" I had learned as a student. This new view was much more scriptural and historical.

Q: What specific authors had been especially important for you at the time?

A: I can remember the names of Congar, Chenu, de Lubac, Rahner, Jungmann, Aubert the historian, Clifford Howell, and John Courtney Murray. Then there was Maritain and finally Teilhard de Chardin, who was the cherry on the top for me. He brought everything together in a magnificent, coherent view of creation and salvation. I think I came across him around 1960. By the time I got to the Central Preparatory Commission I was a real Teilhardian.

Q: Was there a distinction between optimism and pes-

simism, hope and despair, between the conservatives and progressives?

A: What I didn't realize at the time, but did afterward, was that the Church had been on the defensive for four hundred years. There was the Reformation, Galileo and the beginnings of the scientific revolution, the Enlightenment, the Industrial Revolution and the beginnings of the great division between capital and labor, and then socialism and Marxism. All these developments of human culture seemed to be kept at arm's length by the Church. The Church wasn't touching them except to condemn them. I got the impression then that we could go on forever like that.

The progressive cardinals (including Montini, later Pope Paul VI) wanted to get more in touch with the world. That is obviously also what John XXIII had in mind when he spoke of *aggiornamento*. John XXIII was not really a theologian, but he was a well-read person, a deeply spiritual person. I think he had a saintly, spiritual, divine instinct telling him that the Church was out of touch and needed to get back in touch with the world.

Q: Could you describe the workings and dynamics of the Central Preparatory Commission?

A: Other commissions were dealing with various themes of the Council, but there seemed to be no relation between them. They were a scattered collection of themes, which began to come to us one by one. We began, so to speak, at the end. There was no order to it, and I was extremely perplexed.

This question of order came to a head when Cardinal Suenens came to the first meeting of the Central Preparatory Commission early in 1962 (he had just been named Archbishop of Brussels-Malines). Suenens just sat and observed. At the second session in March 1962, I think, he made a very powerful appeal for some order. He proposed an order, beginning with the Church as the central theme, then dealing with the Church *ad intra*—various aspects of the Church like hierarchy, laity, liturgy, Scripture, and so on—and then the Church *ad extra.* That was the first mention, the conception you might say, of *Gaudium et Spes.* I went straight round to him right after that meeting and said, "Congratulations! Now I'm beginning to see some light. You've brought light and order to what we're trying to discuss here." But it made very little difference at the time.

In May that year I was in despair. I thought we would never get this Council off the ground. Nobody paid any attention to the ideas Cardinal Suenens had put forward. We just drifted along from unrelated topic to unrelated theme. When I returned to South Africa after a meeting in June, however, I had some encouragement. I read the schema that had been prepared on the liturgy. I thought "Finally, one good paper!" That was because of the secretary at the time, Hannibal Bugnini. He did a marvelous job. He got together the best liturgists from Europe and America and other countries and picked their brains to prepare a text. A magnificent text it was! That was why the bishops began the Council with the text on liturgy. Apart from that, I was very much in despair, with not much confidence in the Holy Spirit to pull it all together.

Q: You were present on October 11, 1962. How do you remember the opening of the Council?

A: It was a magnificent sight—the *aula* (the nave of Saint Peter's) curtained off, with the seating mounting up on either side and the presidential accommodation in the sanctuary just below the altar. I found myself right near the front, near a TV camera. I knew those Roman ceremonies and thought to myself that this was going to last for hours. I hoped that at the end the man would not turn the camera on me and find me sleeping!

Luckily, Pope John XXIII had prepared a really volcanic speech, advising against "the prophets of doom," speaking of the hope of the *aggiornamento,* of bringing the Church up to date. I sat transfixed throughout his homily. It was magnificent. We had faced some of those prophets of doom in the Central Preparatory Commission.

Q: Was there a sense that the pope was struggling within his own curia then?

A: Yes. He never showed it, of course. He was a very re-spectful, kind, paternal man who never had any complaints. But he must have prayed a lot and suffered a lot and hoped a lot and trusted in the Holy Spirit.

I hadn't trusted in the Holy Spirit to put things right, even after Cardinal Suenens had spoken. I was one of those who thought that the opening should have been postponed. In May of that year, I had gone to one cardinal after another and said, "What can we do? We are not ready. It's hopeless. We have no order, no inspiring documents to discuss." They all said, "Yes we realize that. We don't know what to do." Cardinal Suenens had been working on the problem. He was well known to Pope John XXIII, but even he couldn't do anything. I think the pope thought that once the Council got going, the Holy Spirit would take over and let happen what must develop. He had great trust. He was a great man.

Q: What happened to the documents prepared for the session?

A: The Council started with Bugnini's document on the liturgy. That went well. But from there on it was patchy, especially when we got into the schema on the Church. The progressives rejected that out of hand; it was just the old attitudes played out again. It was as though what we had said in the Central Preparatory Commission had had no impact whatsoever.

We went from one disaster to another for the rest of that first period until some people got to Pope John XXIII. He was very ill at this time, but he said, "I realize there is a problem." They persuaded him that there should be a proper organizing committee to prepare a proper program, and that there should be a revision of most of the schemas—all of those remaining anyway. I still have my notes with a huge note "Thank God!" It was about the fifth or sixth of December.

Cardinal Suenens made again the speech he had made earlier in the year in the Central Preparatory Commission proposing the theme of the Church as the central theme—*ad intra* and *ad extra.*

Q: Did something happen in the whole body of bishops during that session that began to bring the assembly together in some direction?

A: An amazing thing happened. The Holy Spirit has its own way of working among the bishops. It worked among them by creating the biggest, most famous, historical adult education project ever held, I think. This was bishops realizing that they had to find out more about the situation.

Theologians, who had been limited in some way in their ministry and in their writing, were there, with us sitting at their feet hearing what they had to say. All over Rome there were these gatherings outside Saint Peter's in the late afternoons and evenings, listening to the Scripture scholars, the historians, the philosophers, and the theologians. It was a wonderful experience, self-organized by the bishops' conferences, a kind of university education on the cheap.

Q: Were the U.S. bishops a key group?

A: Yes, there were so many of them. Like most English-speaking bishops in the world, they didn't know much about the situation that was coming to a head—the need to "aggiornamentize" the Church. In most English-speaking countries at the time, the Church was in good shape. Parishes were flourishing, missions were going well, Catholic schools were operating well, there were lots of vocations to the priesthood and the religious life. What was the problem? So the American bishops had that difficulty, as did most English-speaking bishops, just understanding what the problem was. I was lucky.

Q: Is it true that the document describing the liturgy as the "source and summit" of the Church, the document that set the tone for the whole Council, was passed almost by accident, simply because it was the best prepared document?

A: Accident? Not exactly, but to go back to the real beginning of the Council, there was some excitement: the election of the Council commissions, who had to see the documents through. It was proposed that we simply let those who had served on the commissions that had prepared the documents play the follow-through role as well.

But there was a bit of a conspiracy. I was a member of it. Congar was very much a part of it, and others like him. Cardinal Lienart of Lille was to stand up before the election got underway and propose that we could not elect commission members without knowing more about them. I knew he was going to do that. After the election was announced there was, as far as I was concerned, an agonizing pause. Bishops around me were going ahead, putting names on their ballots, and I wondered when Lienart was going to speak. Finally we heard his voice. Immediately he was backed by Cardinal Frings—a Franco-German alliance—and there was a burst of applause.

Cardinal Tisserant, an old army sergeant major, I believe, was in charge that day. There was a hurried consultation at the presidential table, which was concluded when it was announced: Take three days off to work out your names for the commissions. We streamed out of Saint Peter's two hours before we were due to leave. People asked, "What is happening? Have you finished the Council already?" That was a very decisive moment. Some very good people were chosen for the theological commission. There was no commission for *Gaudium et Spes* at that stage. It came much later.

Q: As you went home from that first session, how were you feeling?

A: I was excited. I just couldn't stop talking about it. I gave many talks in my diocese and got people all keyed up and warmed up about the Council. Some people at least. It was very exciting. We had picked up the Council and were going through with it.

One of the greatest astonishments I experienced was finding out what brilliant bishops Latin America had. I was very impressed by them. I remember Henrique Silva from Chile, another bishop who was killed in a motor accident, Helder Camara, and Cardinal Lorscheider from Brazil. I knew nothing about the Church in Latin America. Neither Asia nor Africa was very impressive, and the North Americans were just finding their feet in the first session.

I had been elected to the commission dealing with the training of aspirants to the priesthood and with Catholic education. In regard to training for the priesthood, first off I found myself strongly advocating much greater attention to pastoral training. In regard to aspects of formation the tendency was to begin with spiritual formation but I was saying, "For goodness sake, until you can define what kind of person you are trying to produce, how can you talk about the spirituality?" It was difficult. I was almost a lone voice in discussions of this kind.

Q: Let's move to the second session.

A: Of course, the pope died in June 1963, before the second session could convene. There was some uncertainty about whether the Council would continue under the new pope. Yet Cardinal Montini had always been in favor of the Council. He was very much on the side of the progressive cardinals and bishops.

The second session convened in September. We began to work on the document on the Church. We spent the whole month of October arguing about primacy and collegiality. It went on day after day. It was a very difficult subject and the text of the final document clearly shows that you can't really clarify it. So much depends on the primate to call the college together and trust the college. The document that emerged, *Lumen Gentium,* was a key document in the relationship between Vatican I and Vatican II. There was a sense among us that we were completing the work begun in Vatican I.

Q: The sixties was a time when many countries and cultures were struggling with the demands for participation in decision making, a much more collective approach to the process of governing. How much was there a sense of fostering collegiality as a whole style of Church?

A: That was coming through emotionally, the feeling as we talked together. We had great hopes that we would have a very different approach to Church governance. We were not going through the same cultural revolution in South Africa as in other parts of the world. We read about it but didn't experience it. The bishops in Europe must have been much more aware of it. In hindsight, we can see that it was a very important decade in the history of humanity.

At the North American College someone organized a teaching session for the American bishops led by Father Barnabas Ahern, the Passionist biblical scholar. He spoke about the infancy narratives in the Gospel. The apostolic delegate, Archbishop Vagnozzi, was very angry. He came down the steps of that tiered hall and upbraided Barnabas for being among those who were ruining the faith of the simple people of the Church and disturbing religious communities. Barnabas took it humbly and said, "Your Excellency, that's a very good question."

Q: Was the direction now set, once you went through the document on the Church?

A: Yes, now we knew the essential stance that was being taken. As we went on into 1964 and the subsequent session, it got a bit heavy. Many detailed schemas had to be discussed. Some were getting rather boring. The excitement of the early days had died down somewhat. We came back to life with a huge explosion. On a certain day I happened to walk into Saint Peter's with Father John Courtney Murray, a *peritus*. He was downhearted because the Council seemed to be falling asleep; there wasn't much light. We were discussing the ministry of bishops at that time.

Cardinal Frings of Cologne took the opportunity to address the body. He had very bad eyes and huge notes. He spoke slowly, ponderously, with Teutonic consideration for what he was saying. As he began to speak, everybody edged toward the front of their seats, everybody sat up. Frings was criticizing the Holy Office! The atmosphere became electric. We all looked down at the list of speakers for the day and two or three places lower on the list was Cardinal Ottaviani, top man after the Holy Father on the Holy Office. Nobody stirred. At other times people were always dashing off to the two coffee bars, Bar Jonah and Bar Abbas. Not now. We were all waiting for the response of Cardinal Ottaviani.

It was a furious, magnificent response. He came down the steps to the microphone, full sail—his garments floating behind him. I think his first words were something like: "*Altissime protestor-r-r....*" (his r's rolling in fine Italian style). He was protesting furiously what had been said. I think he maintained that anybody who touches the Holy Office touches the Holy Father. We were listening carefully but we were all confused by the excitement of the moment. He gave a rip-roaring response and, though applause was forbidden (actually every now and then some applause did break out), he got a great round of applause—for his style, not for the content. Nobody was reacting to the content, but we all appreciated the style. It reminded me of the line in the old English poem that, "Even the ranks of Tuscany could not forbear to cheer when Horatio kept the bridge." It was a very exciting day. I met John Courtney Murray later that day and he was all smiles.

Q: Hadn't Pope John XXIII's decision not to give the Holy Office responsibility for the conduct of the Council been a blow to the Holy Office?

A: Yes. I had the impression during the discussions in the

Central Preparatory Commission that Cardinal Ottaviani had found it very difficult to accept and to realize emotionally and experientially that the Council was above the Holy Office.

Q: It is said that some of the documents were compromises, containing within them varying theologies in juxtaposition, a step necessary to reach consensus. Is that a fair characterization?

A: I think so. It's not always easy to reach complete unanimity in a gathering of that size—over two thousand bishops. By this time things were moving toward *Gaudium et Spes* and the establishment of a commission to promote it.

While there were moments of intense discussion where important differences among the bishops remained—the dispute over two sources of revelation was one—much of the work of the Council was about the internal life of the Church and was not always so inspiring. *Gaudium et Spes* and the *Decree on Religious Liberty* were important exceptions. *Gaudium et Spes* itself was a bit hurried. It came late and we had to move through it quickly. Poor Father Tucci, the Jesuit who worked on the document, was exhausted trying to include all the amendments at night after a day's work. We did see that *Gaudium et Spes* was needed in addition to *Lumen Gentium* as a statement of the Church. We couldn't do without *Gaudium et Spes.* There were strong feelings in Europe for the need for a definition of the Church's attitude toward society and its role in society.

The decree on freedom of religion did not get through till the very last day of the Council. I found it so hard to understand the difficulty of accepting it, but obviously it was a case of difference of experience between people who lived in a multi-denominational or multi-religious country and those who didn't, those who lived in a largely Catholic country like Italy or Spain.

In the modern world, how could one say that the state must support the one true Church? To me that was ridiculous—how could South Africa ever support the Catholic Church, a tiny minority of the population?

Of course, Cardinal Ottaviani was sold on the other position. Books had been withdrawn from publication just before the Council because they had maintained the opposite opinion. I remember bringing a book from South Africa with me as I passed through Tanzania. A priest there saw the book I had. It was in French, an account of a discussion on freedom of religion that had been held somewhere in France. He said, "It's the very thing I need. I have to advise the bishops of Tanzania on the eve of Tanzania's independence. Please give this to me." "I can't; I borrowed it from the seminary library in South Africa and must return it there." "But you're going to Europe where you can get hundreds of copies of this book."

So I gave in and let him have the book, thinking that I could get a new copy in Europe. But when I got there I couldn't find a copy. They had all been withdrawn. I got to England where I happened to be at a meeting with an editor from Sheed and Ward and mentioned my problem. Then editor said to me, "We've got two thousand copies of the English translation. We can't sell them to you but I can give you one."

Q: Could you speak a little about the leadership of Paul VI in the Council?

A: He was more withdrawn than John XXIII, but he had great determination and great courage. Paul VI was determined to see the Council through and to accept the reforms that were being described. So it was providential. He picked up the Council and went with it—except when it came to the famous issue of birth control, which he withdrew from discussion. We were not allowed to discuss that at the Council.

Q: The Council was an expression of collegiality, not only with the pope but among the bishops. You were one bishop who felt the practical need to practice collegiality regarding the translations of the liturgy into the vernacular. Would you describe the founding of ICEL (International Commission on English in the Liturgy)?

A: As soon as the possibility began to emerge that we would have vernacular languages in the liturgy, I began to fear for the future of a small Catholic population like that of South Africa, which would be bombarded with publications coming from America, England, Ireland, Scotland, and Australia. We would have no control over texts. I don't know how I drifted into a circle consisting of Archbishop Hallinan of Atlanta, Archbishop Grimshaw of Birmingham, and a very strong promoter of the idea of a single translation, Guilford Young of Hobart, Tasmania, in Australia. Also, I was in contact with Fred McManus of the U.S., who was interested. We began to talk about the possibility of a common translation for all English-speaking countries.

We had our final little pre-foundation gathering near the altar of Saint Josaphat in Saint Peter's, that is, the four bishops. We decided to have a meeting in the English College, bringing together representatives of English-speaking countries. When we went back to our places, Archbishop Pericle Felici, the secretary of the Council, chose that time to say that there were too many bishops absenting themselves from the discussions and talking too loudly outside the *aula*. I do not think we added to that disorder.

Hallinan put forward the name of Archbishop Grimshaw as the chairman of our group. This was a bit of a mistake.

Grimshaw had taken care of the translation of the Roman ritual into English. That seemed to fill his mind and heart with contentment. He hardly saw the need to go ahead and prepare for the future. So it was a bit difficult having a chairman like that. We finally got going in 1964. But some of us were afraid that 1964 would be the final session—they were rushing to get things through—and Archbishop Grimshaw was very slow in calling the first meeting of the English-speaking bishops to take up this new proposal.

Finally it came and we got it going. Certainly, Fred McManus played a very big part in it. Godfrey Diekmann was a great supporter. We also had an Irish priest, the editor of the Irish journal called *The Furrow,* who was very helpful too, and an English Jesuit, an outspoken and creative man educated on the continent, Father Clifford Howell. When the liturgy document finally went through, some of us had a dinner to celebrate its approval. To Father Howell we raised our glasses and said, "You now go back to England in triumph." He replied, "No, no! People will forgive you for being wrong, but never for being right."

Q: Have you any reflections on ICEL's history from then to now?

A: ICEL has gone through a number of secretaries. Our first secretary, Father Sigler, was a rather combative type. I remember that the Catholic Truth Society in England published our first translations of the eucharistic prayers without observing the sense lines. Our secretary wanted to sue Cardinal Heenan, the head of the Society. We had another secretary for a short time, then came Father Rotelle who served for several years, and after that Dr. John Page, who has been with us for many years. John has been a wonderful secretary—gentlemanly, hard working, a good planner and organizer, and excellent in creating a good spirit among his staff. We owe a lot to him.

We have had a very fraternal relationship. There were three groups: the bishops elected by their conferences, the officials of ICEL, and the translators and liturgical advisors. We had no difficulty getting along together. Although the bishops had to make the final decisions, we always did so in the light of the discussion and the proposals put before us. We exercised our episcopal authority in a very collegial, friendly, and fraternal way. It was delightful group to work with, a happy group.

Q: How do you account for the controversy of the last few years [of the 1990s]? What changed?

A: It is hard to say. Suddenly the Holy See in the person of Cardinal Medina Estevez decided that our translations were too liberal, too unliteral. These translations have been inspired by a document drawn up by a body known by the Latin name *Concilium Liturgicam.* The document became known by its first three words in French, *Comme il prévoit.* We worked in terms of that. It pointed out very clearly that translations are a difficult job. It is very hard to get exact translations from one language to another. But you must make your translation conform to the spirit and atmosphere of your own language so that it is acceptable and understandable to the people. That was very much the tone of the document. Suddenly we were told that the document had been withdrawn. But no document has replaced it for four years.

All vernacular translations have to be submitted for what is called the *recognitio* of the Holy See. ICEL does not itself submit documents but provides them to bishops' conferences, which in turn apply for the *recognitio.* No great difficulties had been experienced until out of the blue the translation of the revision of the ordination rites came back with well over a hundred corrections.

We realized that there was a new spirit, a new feeling in Rome. I can't understand it. Here we have the finest, devoted workers with knowledge of English, knowledge of the liturgy, and expertise in translation. You could hardly find a better body anywhere in the world. But the Holy See finds a few people, unnamed, who are critical of the ICEL translation and determined to "improve" upon it. It is beyond my understanding.

Q: It has been said that Rome's preoccupation with English translations is because English has become the universal language of the Church and that those speaking other languages translate texts from the English rather than from the Latin. Consequently, Rome feels a propriety right regarding the English. What do you think?

A: It is true that, when you are translating one language removed, it is hard to be sure that you have it right. But we were willing to provide every safeguard. In translating, the last draft for approval by the bishops' conferences would be set out in three columns: the Latin, an almost word-for-word translation, and the recommended ICEL translation. Those who would be translating from the English would have two columns to work from. It is just so sad that there is a lack of trust now in the magnificent men who give their labors and their time with so much care for the work they did, and always with such harmony and with such a spirit of dedication to ICEL.

Q: To bring up another area of collegiality, were the triennial synods of bishops in Rome meant to be a kind of permanent Council? If not, where are the instruments to ensure continuing collegiality?

A: Pope Paul VI, in initiating the triennial synods of bishops in Rome, said that they were not experiences of collegiality. The synods were advisory to the pope. The big failure, as far as I am concerned, is that scholars are not at synods. Without them we do not achieve much. There have been some great synods, such as the synod on evangelization, but in general they lack the input of a scholarly presence.

Dimensions of the Church must meet face to face in exchange: the episcopal dimension and the scholarly dimension. Without the scholarly dimension we are handicapped. I have the greatest respect for the scholars as I saw how well they worked. They respected the episcopal position, and the bishops respected their position.   There were wonderful exchanges, fraternal exchanges, between us.   It is a great pity that the scholars are now seen more as revolutionaries in the Church. Not many are.   In general they are just anxious to push the Church into new areas where it needs to evangelize.

As for an instrument of continuing collegiality, I'd like to see an ecumenical Council held every twenty five years to give every generation of bishops the experience of a Council and to keep pace with the developments of human culture. Without that, collegiality is left to the workings of the individual conferences of bishops around the world.   No universal collegiality is maintained. It is a sad lack in the Catholic Church. When you compare us with other churches, they come together more than we do.

Meanwhile the whole experience of globalization makes some kind of worldwide collegiality essential for the Church. Globalization is going to increase and intensify, leaving the essential reactions of the whole Catholic Church behind. The irony is that no institution is better able to address value questions on a global level than the Catholic Church.   Yet the collegiality that was so rich and full at the Council seems to have dissipated. I sympathize with the bishops who have come after me—a generation after me—and have had no experience of the Council. It is such a great experience. It gives such vitality, such vision, such impetus to the life of the Church.

Q: Looking back at the Council, were there missed opportunities, matters not addressed?

A: As I look back at Vatican II, I think that one of our weaknesses is that we in the Catholic Church rely too much on documents—on encyclicals and pastoral letters. Effects are achieved by getting among the people and getting the people to do things. Cardinal Cardijn taught us that in a magnificent manner. His method has been sadly neglected in the Church— the "see, judge, and act" method. I once lectured in Australia and said that there should be a moratorium on papal encyclicals to give us time to see how to implement them. The documents need to be seen as something to be put into practice, not just read and discussed.

Q: If Pope John Paul II were to call a new Council, what would you suggest for the agenda?

A: It is difficult to answer that question off the cuff. However, my first suggestion is that we should deal with the difficulty experienced by so many people today, the difficulty of accepting the teaching of the Church. The secular mentality seems to override the sacred mentality. We ought to ask the scholars to work on that. It may produce results that will be quite shocking to us. We may not be using the right methods for some reason or another. It's a question of getting back to practical application, practical pursuit of achievement, one of the great weaknesses in the Church.

Then there is the continuation and ongoing exploration and application of the social teaching of the Church. Society is moving so fast these days that we need teaching to keep pace with it, regarding developments like globalization. We all do a little for the poor, but the problem of poverty around the world is so huge today that there should be a great intensification of the Church's conscience about that—of the pope and cardinals, bishops, priests, religious, and laity. One has the impression that in the early Church care of the poor was almost as important as the sacraments. We ought to get back to that again, I think.

Q: What do you think was the greatest achievement of the Council?

A: Its vision of the Church—what the Church is and what it must be in the world. The key to that vision was the presence of the Holy Spirit in the people, in individuals and communities, and the living out of that reality in terms of the culture in which we find ourselves, and the needs of that culture and the needs of that society. [NOTE: This interview has been slightly edited by J. Kroeger; it first appeared in *Church* (Spring 2001): 17-24; reprint permission through FABC.]

5

POPE JOHN'S OPENING SPEECH TO THE COUNCIL

Mother Church rejoices that, by the singular gift of Divine Providence, the longed-for day has finally dawned when—under the auspices of the Virgin Mother of God, whose maternal dignity is commemorated on this feast—the Second Vatican Ecumenical Council is being solemnly opened here beside Saint Peter's tomb.

Ecumenical Councils of the Church. The Councils—both the twenty ecumenical ones and the numberless others, also important, of a provincial or regional character which have been held down through the years—all prove clearly the vigor of the Catholic Church and are recorded as shining lights in her annals. In calling this vast assembly of bishops, the latest and humble successor to the Prince of the Apostles who is addressing you intended to assert once again the magisterium (teaching authority), which is unfailing and endures until the end of time, in order that this magisterium, taking into account the errors, the requirements, and the opportunities of our time, might be presented in exceptional form to all people throughout the world.

It is but natural that in opening this Universal Council we should like to look to the past and to listen to its voices whose echo we like to hear in the memories and the merits of the more recent and ancient Pontiffs, our predecessors. These are solemn and venerable voices, throughout the East and the West, from the fourth century to the Middle Ages, and from there to modern times, which have handed down their witness to those Councils. They are voices which proclaim in perennial fervor the triumph of that divine and human institution, the Church of Christ, which from Jesus takes its name, its grace, and its meaning.

Side by side with these motives for spiritual joy, however, there has also been for more than nineteen centuries a cloud of sorrows and of trials. Not without reason did the ancient Simeon announce to Mary the Mother of Jesus, that prophecy which has been and still is true: "Behold this child is set for the fall and the rise of many in Israel, and for a sign which shall be contradicted" (Lk. 2:34). And Jesus Himself, when He grew up, clearly outlined the manner in which the world would treat His person down through the succeeding centuries with the mysterious words: "He who hears you, hears me" (Lk. 10:16), and with those others that the same evangelist relates: "He who is not with me is against me and he who does not gather with me scatters" (Lk. 11:23).

The great problem confronting the world after almost two thousand years remains unchanged. Christ is ever resplendent as the center of history and of life. People are either with Him and His Church, and then they enjoy light, goodness, order, and peace. Or else, they are without Him, or against Him, and deliberately opposed to His Church, and then they give rise to confusion, to bitterness in human relations, and to the constant dangers of fratricidal wars.

Ecumenical Councils, whenever they are assembled, are a solemn celebration of the union of Christ and His Church, and hence lead to the universal radiation of truth, to the proper guidance of individuals in domestic and social life, to the strengthening of spiritual energies for a perennial uplift toward real and everlasting goodness.

The testimony of this extraordinary magisterium of the Church in the succeeding epochs of these twenty centuries of Christian history stands before us collected in numerous and imposing volumes, which are the sacred patrimony of our ecclesiastical archives, here in Rome and in the more noted libraries of the entire world.

Origin and Reason for the Second Vatican Ecumenical Council. As regards the initiative for the great event which gathers us here, it will suffice to repeat as historical documentation our personal account of the first sudden bringing up in our heart and lips of the simple words: "Ecumenical Council." We uttered those words in the presence of the Sacred College of Cardinals on that memorable January 25, 1959, the feast of the Conversion of Saint Paul, in the basilica dedicated to him. It was completely unexpected, like a flash of heavenly light, shedding sweetness in eyes and hearts. And at the same time, it gave rise to a great fervor throughout the world in expectation of the holding of the Council.

There have elapsed three years of laborious preparation, during which a wide and profound examination was made regarding modern conditions of faith and religious practice, and of Christian and especially Catholic vitality. These years have seemed to us a first sign, an initial gift of celestial grace.

Illuminated by the light of this Council, the Church—we confidently trust—will become greater in spiritual riches and gaining the strength of new energies therefrom, she will look to the future without fear. In fact, by bringing herself up to date where required, and by the wise organization of mutual cooperation, the Church will make all families and peoples really turn their minds to heavenly things.

And thus, the holding of the Council becomes a motive for wholehearted thanksgiving to the Giver of every good gift, in order to celebrate with joyous canticles the glory of Christ our Lord, the glorious and immortal King of ages and of peoples.

The opportuneness of holding the Council is, moreover, venerable brothers, another subject which it is useful to propose for your consideration. Namely, in order to render our joy more complete, we wish to narrate before this great assembly our assessment of the happy circumstances under which the Ecumenical Council commences.

In the daily exercise of our pastoral office, we sometimes have to listen, much to our regret, to voices of persons who, though burning with zeal, are not endowed with too much sense of discretion or measure. In these modern times they can see nothing but prevarication and ruin. They say that our era, in comparison with past eras, is getting worse, and they behave as though they had learned nothing from history, which is, none the less, the teacher of life. They behave as though at the time of former Councils everything was a full triumph for the Christian idea and life and for proper religious liberty.

We feel must disagree with those prophets of gloom, who are always forecasting disaster, as though the end of the world were at hand. In the present order of things, Divine Providence is leading us to a new order of human relations which, by people's own efforts and even beyond their very expectations, are directed toward the fulfillment of God's superior and inscrutable designs. And everything, even human differences, leads to the greater good of the Church.

It is easy to discern this reality if we consider attentively the world of today, which is so busy with politics and controversies in the economic order that it does not find time to attend to the care of spiritual reality, with which the Church's magisterium is concerned. Such a way of acting is certainly not right, and must justly be disapproved. It cannot be denied, however, that these new conditions of modern life have at least the advantage of having eliminated those innumerable obstacles by which, at one time, the children of this world impeded the free action of the Church. In fact, it suffices to leaf even cursorily through the pages of ecclesiastical history to note clearly how the Ecumenical Councils themselves, while constituting a series of true glories for the Catholic Church, were often held to the accompaniment of most serious difficulties and sufferings because of the undue interference of civil authorities.   The princes of this world, indeed, sometimes in all sincerity, intended thus to protect the Church. But more frequently, this occurred not without spiritual damage and danger, since their interest therein was guided by the views of a selfish and perilous policy.

In this regard, we confess to you that we feel most poignant sorrow over the fact that very many bishops, so dear to us, are noticeable here today by their absence, because they are imprisoned for their faithfulness to Christ or impeded by other restraints. The thought of them impels us to raise most fervent prayer to God. Nevertheless, we see today, not without great hopes and to our immense consolation, that the Church, finally freed from so many obstacles of a profane nature such as trammeled her in the past, can from this Vatican Basilica, as if from a second apostolic cenacle, and through your intermediary, raise her voice resonant with majesty and greatness.

Principle Duty of the Council: Defense and Advancement of Truth. The greatest concern of the Ecumenical Council is this: that the sacred deposit of Christian doctrine should be guarded and taught more efficaciously. That doctrine embraces the whole person, composed of body and soul. And, since humanity is a pilgrim on this earth, it commands people to tend always toward heaven.

This demonstrates how our mortal life is to be ordered in such a way as to fulfill our duties as citizens of earth and of heaven, and thus to attain the aim of life as established by God. That is, all people, whether taken singly or as united in society, today have the duty of tending ceaselessly during their lifetime toward the attainment of heavenly things and to use, for this purpose only, the earthly goods, the employment of which must not prejudice their eternal happiness.

The Lord has said: "Seek first the kingdom of God and his justice" (Mt. 6:33). The word "first" expresses the direction in which our thoughts and energies must move. We must not, however, neglect the other words of this exhortation of our Lord, namely: "And all these things shall be given you besides" (Mt. 6:33). In reality, there always have been in the Church, and there are still today, those who, while seeking the practice of evangelical perfection with all their might, do not fail to make themselves useful to society. Indeed, it is from their constant example of life and their charitable undertakings that all that is highest and noblest in human society takes its strength and growth.

In order, however, that this doctrine may influence the numerous fields of human activity, with reference to individuals, to families, and to social life, it is necessary first of all that the Church should never depart from the sacred patrimony of truth received from the Fathers. But, at the same time, she must ever look to the present, to the new conditions and new forms of life introduced into the modern world, which have opened new avenues to the Catholic apostolate.

For this reason, the Church has not watched inertly the marvelous progress of the discoveries of human genius, and has not been backward in evaluating them rightly. But, while following these developments, she does not neglect to admonish people so that, over and above the sensible—perceived things—they may raise their eyes to God, the Source of all wisdom and all beauty. And may they never forget the most serious command: "The Lord thy God shall thou worship, and Him only shall thou serve" (Mt. 4:10; Lk. 4:8), so that it happens that the fleeting fascination of visible things should impede true progress.

As to the manner in which sacred doctrine is spread, this having been established, it becomes clear how much is expected from the Council in regard to doctrine. That is, the Twenty-first Ecumenical Council, which will draw upon the effective and important wealth of juridical, liturgical, apostolic, and administrative experiences, wishes to transmit the doctrine, pure and integral, without any attenuation or distortion, which throughout twenty centuries, notwithstanding difficulties and contrasts, has become the common patrimony of humanity. It is a patrimony not well received by all, but always a rich treasure available to people of good will.

Our duty is not only to guard this precious treasure, as if we were concerned only with antiquity, but to dedicate ourselves with an earnest will and without fear to that work which our era demands of us, pursuing thus the path which the Church has followed for twenty centuries. The salient point of this Council is not, therefore, a discussion of one article or another of the fundamental doctrine of the Church which has repeatedly been taught by the Fathers and by ancient and modern theologians, and which is presumed to be well known and familiar.

For this a Council was not necessary. But from the renewed, serene, and tranquil adherence to all the teaching of the Church in its entirety and preciseness, as it still shines forth in the Acts of the Council of Trent and First Vatican Council, the Christian, Catholic, and apostolic spirit of the whole world expects a step forward toward a doctrinal penetration and a formation of consciousness in faithful and perfect conformity to the authentic doctrine, which, however, should be studied and expounded through the methods of research and through the literary forms of modern thought. The substance of the ancient doctrine of the deposit of faith is one thing, and the way in which it is presented is another. And it is the latter that must be taken into great consideration with patience if necessary, everything being measured in the forms and proportions of a magisterium which is predominantly pastoral in character.

How to Repress Errors. At the outset of the Second Vatican Council, it is evident, as always, that the truth of the Lord will remain forever. We see, in fact, as one age succeeds another, that human opinions follow one another and exclude each other. And, often errors vanish as quickly as they arise, like fog before the sun.

The Church has always opposed these errors. Frequently she has condemned them with the greatest severity. Nowadays however, the Spouse of Christ prefers to make use of the medicine of mercy rather than that of severity. She considers that she meets the needs of the present day by demonstrating the validity of her teaching rather than by condemnations. Not, certainly, that there is a lack of fallacious teaching, opinions, and dangerous concepts to be guarded against and dissipated. But these are so obviously in contrast with the right norm of honesty, and have produced such lethal fruits that by now it would seem that people of themselves are inclined to condemn them, particularly those ways of life which despise God and His law or place excessive confidence in technical progress and a well-being based exclusively on the comforts of life. They are ever more deeply convinced of the paramount dignity of the human person and of his perfection as well as of the duties which that implies. Even more important, experience has taught humanity that violence inflicted on others, the might of arms, and political domination, are of no help at all in finding a happy solution to the grave problems which afflict them.

That being so, the Catholic Church, raising the torch of religious truth by means of this Ecumenical Council, desires to show herself to be the loving mother of all, benign, patient, full of mercy and goodness toward the brethren who are separated from her. To humankind, oppressed by so many difficulties, the Church says, as Peter said to the poor who begged alms from him: "I have neither gold nor silver, but what I have I give you; in the name of Jesus Christ of Nazareth, rise and walk" (Acts 3:6). In other words, the Church does not offer to the people of today riches that pass, nor does she promise them merely earthly happiness. But she distributes to them the goods of divine grace which, raising all to the dignity of children of God, are the most efficacious safeguards and aids toward a more human life. She opens the fountain of her life-giving doctrine which allows people, enlightened by the light of Christ, to understand well what they really are, what their lofty dignity and their purpose are, and, finally, through her children, she spreads everywhere the fullness of Christian charity; nothing is more effective in eradicating the seeds of discord, nothing more efficacious in promoting concord, just peace, and the human unity of all.

Unity of the Christian and Human Family Must be Promoted. The Church's solicitude to promote and defend truth derives from the fact that, according to the plan of God, who wills all to be saved and to come to the knowledge of the truth (I Tim. 2:4), persons without the assistance of the whole of revealed doctrine cannot reach a complete and firm unity of minds, with which are associated true peace and eternal salvation. Unfortunately, the entire Christian family has not yet attained this unity in truth.

The Catholic Church, therefore, considers it her duty to work actively so that there may be fulfilled the great mystery of that unity, which Jesus Christ invoked with fervent prayer from His heavenly Father on the eve of His sacrifice. She rejoices in peace, knowing well that she is intimately associated with that prayer, and then exults greatly at seeing that invocation extend its efficacy with salutary fruit, even among those who are outside her fold.

Indeed, if one considers well this same unity which Christ implored for His Church, it seems to shine, as it were, with a triple ray of beneficent supernal light: namely, the unity of Catholics among themselves, which must always be kept exemplary and most firm; the unity of prayers and ardent desires with which those Christians separated from this Apostolic See aspire to be united with us; and the unity in esteem and respect for the Catholic Church which animates those who follow non-Christian religions.

In this regard, it is a source of considerable sorrow to see that the greater part of the human race—although all who are born were redeemed by the blood of Christ—does not yet participate in those sources of divine grace which exist in the Catholic Church. Hence the Church, whose light illumines all, whose strength of supernatural unity redounds to the advantage of all humanity, is rightly described in these beautiful words of Saint Cyprian: "The Church, surrounded by divine light, spreads her rays over the entire earth. This light, however, is one and unique and shines everywhere without causing any separation in the unity of the body. She extends her branches over the whole world. By her fruitfulness she sends ever farther afield her rivulets. Nevertheless, the head is always one, the origin one for she is the one mother, abundantly fruitful. We are born of her, are nourished by her milk, we live of her spirit" (*De Catholicae Eccles. Unitate* 5).

Venerable brothers, such is the aim of the Second Vatican Ecumenical Council, which, while bringing together the Church's best energies and striving to have all welcome more favorably the good tidings of salvation, prepares, as it were, and consolidates the path toward that unity of humankind which is required as a necessary foundation, in order that the earthly city may be brought to the resemblance of that heavenly city where truth reigns, charity is the law, and whose extent is eternity (cf. Saint Augustine, *Epistle* 138, 3).

Now, "our voice is directed to you" (2 Cor. 6:11) venerable brothers in the episcopate. Behold, we are gathered together in this Vatican Basilica, upon which hinges the history of the Church, where heaven and earth are closely joined, here near the tomb of Peter and near so many of the tombs of our holy predecessors, whose ashes in this solemn hour seem to thrill in mystic exultation.

The Council now beginning rises in the Church like daybreak, a forerunner of most splendid light. It is now only dawn. And already at this first announcement of the rising day, how much sweetness fills our heart. Everything here breathes sanctity and arouses great joy. Let us contemplate the stars, which with their brightness augment the majesty of this temple. These stars, according to the testimony of the Apostle John (Rev. 1:20), are you, and with you we see shining around the tomb of the Prince of the Apostles, the golden candelabra, that is, the Church confided to you (Rev. 1:20).

We see here with you important personalities, present in an attitude of great respect and cordial expectation, having come together in Rome from the five continents to represent the nations of the world.

We might say that heaven and earth are united in the holding of the Council—the saints of heaven to protect our work, the faithful of the earth continuing in prayer to the Lord, and you, seconding the inspiration of the Holy Spirit in order that the work of all may correspond to the modern expectations and needs of the various peoples of the world. This requires of you serenity of mind, brotherly concord, moderation in proposals, dignity in discussion, and wisdom of deliberation. God grant that your labors and your work, toward which the eyes of all peoples and the hopes of the entire world are turned, may abundantly fulfill the aspirations of all.

Almighty God! In Thee we place all our confidence, not trusting in our own strength. Look down benignly upon these pastors of Thy Church. May the light of Thy supernal grace aid us in taking decisions and in making laws. Graciously hear the prayers which we pour forth to Thee in unanimity of faith, of voice, and of mind.

O Mary, Help of Christians, Help of Bishops, of whose love we have recently had particular proof in thy temple of Loreto, where we venerated the mystery of the Incarnation, dispose all things for a happy and propitious outcome, with thy spouse, Saint Joseph, the holy Apostles Peter and Paul, Saint John the Baptist and Saint John the Evangelist, interceding for us to God.

To Jesus Christ, our most amiable Redeemer, immortal King of peoples and of times, be love, power, and glory forever and ever.

NOTE: On October 11, 1962, the first day of the Second Vatican Council, Pope John XXIII delivered this address in Saint Peter's Basilica; it is often known by its opening words *Gaudet Mater Ecclesia* [Mother Church Rejoices].

6

MESSAGE TO HUMANITY FROM COUNCIL FATHERS

The Fathers of the Council to All Humanity. We take great pleasure in sending to all people and nations a message concerning that well-being, love, and peace which were brought into the world by Christ Jesus, the Son of the living God, and entrusted to the Church.

For this is the reason why, at the direction of the most blessed John XXIII, we successors of the apostles have gathered here, joined in single-hearted prayer with Mary, the Mother of Jesus, and forming one apostolic body headed by the successor of Peter.

May the Face of Christ Jesus Shine Out. In this assembly, under the guidance of the Holy Spirit, we wish to inquire how we ought to renew ourselves, so that we may be found increasingly faithful to the Gospel of Christ. We shall take pains to present to the people of this age God's truth in its integrity and purity that they may understand it and gladly assent to it.

Since we are shepherds, we desire that all those may have their longing satisfied who seek God "if perhaps they might find Him as they grope after Him; though indeed He is not far from each of us" (Acts 17:27).

Hence, obeying the will of Christ, who delivered Himself to death "that He might present to Himself the Church, not having spot or wrinkle ... but that she might be holy and without blemish" (Eph. 5:27), we as pastors devote all our energies and thoughts to the renewal of ourselves and the flocks committed to us, so that there may radiate before all humanity the lovable features of Jesus Christ, who shines in our hearts "that God's splendor may be revealed" (2 Cor. 4:6).

God so Loved the World. We believe that the Father so loved the world that He gave His own Son to save it. Indeed, through this same Son of His He freed us from bondage to sin, reconciling all things unto himself through Him, "making peace through the blood of his cross" (Col. 1:20), so that "we might be called children of God, and truly be such" (cf. Rom. 8:14-17).

The Spirit too has been bestowed on us by the Father, that living the life of God, we might love God and the brethren, who are all of us one in Christ. It is far from true that because we cling to Christ we are diverted from earthly duties and toils. On the contrary, faith, hope, and the love of Christ impel us to serve our brothers, thereby patterning ourselves after the example of the Divine Teacher, who "came not to be served but to serve" (Mt. 20:28). Hence, the Church too was not born to dominate but to serve. He laid down His life for us, and we too ought to lay down our lives for our brothers (1 Jn. 3:16).

Accordingly, while we hope that the light of faith will shine more clearly and more vigorously as a result of this Council's efforts, we look forward to a spiritual renewal from which will also flow a happy impulse on behalf of human values such as scientific discoveries, technological advances, and a wider diffusion of knowledge.

The Love of Christ Impels Us. Coming together in unity

from every nation under the sun, we carry in our hearts the hardships, the bodily and mental distress, the sorrows, longings, and hopes of all the peoples entrusted to us. We urgently turn our thoughts to all the anxieties by which modern humanity is afflicted. Hence, let our concern swiftly focus first of all on those who are especially lowly, poor, and weak. Like Christ, we would have pity on the multitude weighed down with hunger, misery, and lack of knowledge. We want to fix a steady gaze on those who still lack the opportune help to achieve a way of life worthy of human beings.

As we undertake our work, therefore, we would emphasize whatever concerns the dignity of humanity, whatever contributes to a genuine community of peoples. "Christ's love impels us" (2 Cor. 5:14) for "he who sees his brother in need and closes his heart to him, how does the love of God abide in Him?" (1 Jn. 3:17).

Two Issues of Special Urgency Confront Us.   The Supreme Pontiff, John XXIII, in a radio address delivered on September 11, 1962, stressed two points especially. The first dealt with peace between peoples. There is no one who does not hate war, no one who does not strive for peace with burning desire. But the Church desires it most of all, because she is the Mother of all. Through the voice of the Roman Pontiffs, she never ceases to make an open declaration of her love for peace, her desire for peace. She is always ready to lend aid with her whole heart to any sincere effort on behalf of peace. She strives with all her might to bring peoples together and to develop among them a mutual respect for interests and feelings. This very conciliar congress of ours, so impressive in the diversity of races, nations, and languages it represents, does it not bear witness to a community of brotherly love, and shine as a visible sign of it? We are giving witness that all people are brothers and sisters, whatever their race or nation.

The Supreme Pontiff also pleads for social justice. The teaching expounded in his encyclical *Mater et Magistra* clearly shows that the Church is supremely necessary for the modern world if injustices and unworthy inequalities are to be denounced, and if the true order of affairs and of values is to be restored, so that life can become more human according to the standards of the Gospel.

The Power of the Holy Spirit. To be sure, we are lacking in human resources and earthly power. Yet we lodge our trust in the power of God's Spirit, who was promised to the Church by the Lord Jesus Christ. Hence, we humbly and ardently call for all people to work along with us in building up a more just and fraternal city in this world. We call not only upon our brethren whom we serve as shepherds, but also upon all our brother Christians, and the rest of people of good will, whom God "wills that they be saved and come to the knowledge of the truth" (1 Tim. 2:4). For this is the divine plan, that through love God's kingdom may already shine out on earth in some fashion as a preview of God's eternal kingdom.

The world is still far from the desired peace because of threats arising from the very progress of science, marvelous though it be, but not always responsive to the higher law of morality. Our prayer is that in the midst of this world there may radiate the light of our great hope in Jesus Christ, our only Savior.

NOTE: This message to all humanity was issued on October 20, 1962 at the beginning of the Second Vatican Council by the Council Fathers with the endorsement of John XXIII, the Supreme Pontiff.

7

POPE PAUL'S CLOSING SPEECH TO THE COUNCIL

Your eminences, venerable brothers, representatives of governments, gentlemen of the city of Rome, authorities and citizens of the entire world! You, observers belonging to so many different Christian denominations, and you, faithful and sons here present, and you also scattered across the earth and united with us in faith and charity!

You will hear shortly, at the end of this holy Mass, a reading of some messages which, at the conclusion of its work, the Ecumenical Council is addressing to various categories of persons, intending to consider in them the countless forms in which human life finds expression. And you will also hear the reading of our official decree in which we declare terminated and closed the Second Vatican Ecumenical Council. This is a moment, a brief moment of greetings. Then, our voice will be silent. This Council is completely terminated, this immense and extraordinary assembly is disbanded.

Hence, this greeting which we address to you has particular significance, which we take the liberty of pointing out to you, not to distract you from prayer, but to occupy better your attention in this present celebration.

This greeting is, before all, universal. It is addressed to all of you assisting and participating here in this sacred rite: to you, venerable brothers in the episcopate; to you, representatives of nations; to you, people of God. And, it is extended and broadened to the entire world. How could it be otherwise if this Council was said to be and is ecumenical, that is to say, universal? Just as the sound of the bell goes out through the skies, reaching each one within the radius of its sound waves, so at this moment does our greeting go out to each and every one of you. To those who receive it and to those who do not, it resounds pleadingly in the ear of every person. From this Catholic center of Rome, no one, in principle, is unreachable; in principle, all people can and must be reached. For the Catholic Church, no one is a stranger, no one is excluded, no one is far away. Everyone to whom our greeting is addressed is one who is called, who is invited and who, in a certain sense, is present. This is the language of the heart of one who loves. Every loved one is present! And we, especially at this moment, in virtue of our universal pastoral and apostolic mandate, we love all, all humanity.

Hence, we say this to you good and faithful souls who, absent in person from this gathering of believers and of nations, are here present in spirit with your prayer. The Pope is thinking of you too, and with you he celebrates this sublime moment of universal communion.

We say this to you, you who suffer like prisoners of your infirmities, to you who, if you were without the comfort of our heartfelt greeting, would because of your spiritual solitude, experience a redoubling of your pain.

This we say especially to you, brothers in the episcopate, who through no fault of your own were missing from the Council and now leave voids in the ranks of your brother bishops and still more in their hearts and ours, a void which gives us such suffering and which condemns the injustices which shackle your liberty—would that this were all that was wanting to enable you to come to our Council.

Greetings to you, brothers, who are unjustly detained in silence, in oppression, and in the privation of the legitimate and sacred rights owed to every honest person, and much more to you who are the workers of nothing but good, piety and peace. To hindered and humiliated brethren, the Church is with you. She is with your faithful and with all those who have a part in your painful condition! May this also be the civil conscience of the world!

Lastly, our universal greeting goes out to you, those who do not know us, those who do not understand us, those who do not regard us as useful, necessary or friendly. This greeting goes also to you, people who, while perhaps thinking they are doing good, are opposed to us. A sincere greeting, an unassuming greeting, but one filled with hope and, today, please believe that it is filled with esteem and love.

This is our greeting. But please be attentive, you who are listening to us. We ask you to consider how our greetings, differently from what ordinarily happens in day-to-day conversation, would serve to terminate a relationship of nearness or discourse. Our greeting tends to strengthen and, if necessary, to produce a spiritual relationship, whence it draws its meaning and its voice. Ours is a greeting, not of farewell which separates, but of friendship which remains, and which, if so demanded, wishes to be born. It is even precisely in this last expression that our greeting, on the one hand, would desire to reach the heart of every person, to enter therein as a cordial guest, and speak, in the interior silence of your individual souls, the habitual and ineffable words of the Lord: "My peace I leave with you, my peace I give unto you, but not as the world gives it" (Jn. 14:27). Christ has His own special way of speaking in the secrets of hearts. On the other hand, our greeting wants to be a different and higher relationship, because it is not only a two-sided exchange of words among us people of this earth, but it also brings into the picture another one present, the Lord Himself, invisible but working in the framework of human relationships. It invites Him and begs of Him to arouse in him who greets and in him who is greeted new gifts of which the first and highest is charity.

Behold, this is our greeting. May it rise as a new spark of divine charity in our hearts, a spark which may enkindle the principles, doctrine and proposals which the Council has organized and which, thus inflamed by charity, may really produce in the Church and in the world that renewal of thoughts, activities, conduct, moral force, hope and joy which was the very scope of the Council.

Consequently, our greeting is in the ideal order. Is it a dream? Is it poetry? Is it only a conventional and meaningless exaggeration as often happens in our day-to-day expression of good wishes? No. This greeting is ideal, but not unreal. Here we would ask for a further moment of your attention. When we humans push our thoughts and our desires toward an ideal conception of life, we find ourselves immediately in a utopia, in rhetorical caricature, in illusion or delusion. Humanity preserves an unquenchable yearning toward ideal and total perfection, but of itself, it is incapable of reaching it, perhaps not in concept or much less with experience or reality. This we know, it is the drama of humanity, the drama of the fallen king.

But note what is taking place here this morning. While we close the Ecumenical Council, we are honoring Mary Most Holy, the Mother of Christ, and consequently, as we declared on another occasion, the Mother of God and our spiritual mother. We are honoring Mary Most Holy, the Immaculate One, therefore innocent, stupendous, perfect. She is the woman, the true woman who is both ideal and real, the creature in whom the image of God is reflected with absolute clarity, without any disturbance, as happens in every other human creature.

Is it not perhaps in directing our gaze on this woman who is our humble sister and at the same time our heavenly mother and queen, the spotless and sacred mirror of infinite beauty, that we can terminate the spiritual ascent of the Council and our final greeting? Is it not here that our post-conciliar work can begin? Does not the beauty of Mary Immaculate become for us an inspiring model, a comforting hope?

Oh, brothers, sons, and people who are listening to us, we think it is so for us and for you. And this is our most exalted and, God willing, our most valuable greeting.

NOTE: This is the closing address that Pope Paul VI delivered on December 8, 1965, the final day of the Council.

8

CLOSING MESSAGES TO VARIOUS SECTORS OF SOCIETY

Pope Paul VI to the Council Fathers

The hour for departure and separation has sounded. In a few moments you are about to leave the Council assembly to go out to meet humanity and to bring the good news of the Gospel of Christ and of the renovation of His Church, which we have been working at together for four years.

This is a unique moment, a moment of incomparable significance and riches. In this universal assembly, in this privileged point of time and space, there converge together the past, the present and the future: the *past:* for here, gathered in this spot, we have the Church of Christ with her tradition, her history, her councils, her doctors, her saints; the *present:* for we are taking leave of one another to go out to the world of today with its miseries, its sufferings, its sins, but also with its prodigious accomplishment, its values, its virtues; and, lastly, the *future* is here in the urgent appeal of the peoples of the world for more justice, in their will for peace, in their conscious or unconscious thirst for a higher life, that life precisely which the Church of Christ can and wishes to give them.

We seem to hear from every corner of the world an immense and confused voice, the questions of all those who look towards the Council and ask us anxiously: "Have you not a word for us?" For us rulers? For us intellectuals, workers, and artists? And for us women? For us of the younger generation, for us the sick and the poor?

These pleading voices will not remain unheeded. It is for all these categories of people that the Council has been working for four years. It is for them that there has been prepared this *Constitution on the Church in the Modern World*, which we promulgated yesterday amidst the enthusiastic applause of your assembly.

From our long meditation on Christ and His Church there should spring forth at this moment a first announcement of peace and salvation for the waiting multitudes. Before breaking up, the Council wishes to fulfill this prophetic function and to translate into brief messages and in a language accessible to all people, the "good news" which it has for the world and which some of its most respected spokesmen are now about to pronounce in your name for the whole of humanity.

Message to Rulers

At this solemn moment, we, the Fathers of the 21st ecumenical council of the Catholic Church, on the point of disbanding after four years of prayer and work, with the full consciousness of our mission toward humankind, address ourselves respectively and confidently to those who hold in their hands the destiny of people on this earth, to all those who hold temporal power.

We proclaim publicly: We do honor to your authority and your sovereignty, we respect your office, we recognize your just laws, we esteem those who make them and those who apply them. But we have a sacrosanct word to speak to you and it is this: Only God is great. God alone is the beginning and the end. God alone is the source of your authority and the foundation of your laws.

Your task is to be in the world the promoters of order and peace among people. But never forget this: It is God, the living and true God, who is the Father of all. And it is Christ, His eternal Son, who came to make this known to us and to teach us that we are all brothers. He it is who is the great artisan of order and peace on earth, for He it is who guides human history and who alone can incline hearts to renounce those evil passions which beget war and misfortune. It is He who blesses the bread of the human race, who sanctifies its work and its suffering, who gives it those joys which you can never give it, and strengthens it in those sufferings which you cannot console.

In your earthly and temporal city, God constructs mysteriously His spiritual and eternal city, His Church. And what does this Church ask of you after close to 2,000 years of experiences of all kinds in her relations with you, the powers of the earth? What does the Church ask of you today? She tells you in one of the major documents of this Council. She asks of you only liberty, the liberty to believe and to preach her faith, the freedom to love her God and serve Him, the freedom to live and to bring to people her message of life. Do not fear her. She is made after the image of her Master, whose mysterious action does not interfere with your prerogatives but heals everything human of its fatal weakness, transfigures it, and fills it with hope, truth and beauty.

Allow Christ to exercise His purifying action on society. Do not crucify Him anew. This would be a sacrilege for He is the Son of God. This would be suicide for He is the Son of man. And we, His humble ministers, allow us to spread everywhere without hindrance the Gospel of peace on which we have meditated during this Council. Of it, your peoples will be the first beneficiaries, since the Church forms for you loyal citizens, friends of social peace and progress.

On this solemn day when she closes the deliberations of her 21st ecumenical council, the Church offers you through our voice her friendship, her services, her spiritual and moral forces. She addresses to you all her message of salvation and blessing. Accept it, as she offers it to you with a joyous and sincere heart and pass it on to your peoples.

NOTE: This message was read by Achille Cardinal Lienart of Lille, France, assisted by Bernard Cardinal Alfrink of Utrecht, the Netherlands, and Giovanni Cardinal Colombo of Milan, Italy.

Message to Academics and Scientists

A very special greeting to you, seekers after truth, to you, people of thought and science, the explorers of humanity, of the universe and of history, to all of you who are pilgrims enroute to the light and to those also who have stopped along the road, tired and disappointed by their vain search.

Why a special greeting for you? Because all of us here, Bishops and Fathers of the Council, are on the lookout for truth. What have our efforts amounted to during these four years except a more attentive search for and deepening of the message of truth entrusted to the Church and an effort at more perfect docility to the Spirit of truth.

Hence our paths could not fail to cross. Your road is ours. Your paths are never foreign to ours. We are the friends of your vocation as searchers, companions in your fatigues, admirers of your successes and, if necessary, consolers in your discouragement and your failures.

Hence for you also we have a message and it is this: Continue your search without tiring and without ever despairing of the truth. Recall the words of one of your great friends, Saint Augustine: "Let us seek with the desire to find, and find with the desire to seek still more." Happy are those who, while possessing the truth, search more earnestly for it in order to renew it, deepen it, and transmit it to others. Happy also are those who, not having found it, are working toward it with a sincere heart. May they seek the light of tomorrow with the light of today until they reach the fullness of light.

But do not forget that if thinking is something great, it is first a duty. Woe to him who voluntarily closes his eyes to the light. Thinking is also a responsibility, so woe to those who darken the spirit by the thousand tricks which degrade it, make it proud, deceive and deform it. What other basic principle is there for people of science except to think rightly?

For this purpose, without troubling your efforts, without dazzling brilliance, we come to offer you the light of our mysterious lamp which is faith. He who entrusted this lamp to us is the sovereign Master of all thought, He whose humble disciples we are, the only one who said and could have said: "I am the light of the world; I am the way, the truth and the life."

These words have meaning for you. Never perhaps, thank God, has there been so clear a possibility as today of a deep understanding between real science and real faith, mutual servants of one another in the one truth. Do not stand in the way of this important meeting. Have confidence in faith, this great friend of intelligence. Enlighten yourselves with its light in order to take hold of truth, the whole truth. This is the wish, the encouragement and the hope, which, before disbanding, is expressed to you by the Fathers of the entire world assembled at Rome in Council.

NOTE: This message was read by Paul Emile Cardinal Leger of Montreal, assisted by Antonio Cardinal Caggiano of Buenos Aires and Norman Cardinal Gilroy of Sydney, Australia.

Message to Artists

We now address you, artists, who are taken up with beauty and work for it: poets and literary persons, painters, sculptors, architects, musicians, men and women devoted to the theater and the cinema. To all of you, the Church of the Council declares to you through our voice: if you are friends of genuine art, you are our friends.

The Church has long since joined in alliance with you. You have built and adorned her temples, celebrated her dogmas, enriched her liturgy. You have aided her in translating her divine message in the language of forms and figures, making the invisible world palpable. Today, as yesterday, the Church needs you and turns to you. She tells you through our voice: Do not allow an alliance as fruitful as this to be broken. Do not refuse to put your talents at the service of divine truth. Do not close your mind to the breath of the Holy Spirit.

This world in which we live needs beauty in order not to sink into despair. It is beauty, like truth, which brings joy to the human heart and is that precious fruit which resists the wear and tear of time, which unites generations and makes them share things in admiration. And all of this is through your hands. May these hands be pure and disinterested. Remember that you are the guardians of beauty in the world. May that suffice to free you from tastes which are passing and have no genuine value, to free you from the search after strange or unbecoming expressions. Be always and everywhere worthy of your ideals and you will be worthy of the Church which, by our voice, addresses to you today her message of friendship, salvation, grace and benediction.

NOTE: This statement was read by Leo Cardinal Suenens of Malines-Brussels, Belgium, assisted by Lawrence Cardinal Shehan of Baltimore and Jaime Cardinal de Barros Camara of Rio de Janeiro.

Message to Women

And now it is to you that we address ourselves: women of all states—girls, wives, mothers and widows, to you also, consecrated virgins and women living alone—you constitute half of the immense human family. As you know, the Church is proud to have glorified and liberated woman, and in the course of the centuries, in diversity of characters, to have brought into relief her basic equality with men. But the hour is coming, in fact has come, when the vocation of woman is being achieved in its fullness, the hour in which woman acquires in the world an influence, an effect and a power never hitherto achieved. That is why, at this moment when the human race is undergoing so deep a transformation, women impregnated with the spirit of the Gospel can do so much to aid humankind in not falling.

You women have always had as your lot the protection of the home, the love of beginnings and an understanding of cradles. You are present in the mystery of a life beginning. You offer consolation in the departure of death. Our technology runs the risk of becoming inhuman. Reconcile humans with life and above all, we beseech you, watch carefully over the future of our race. Hold back the hand of those who, in a moment of folly, might attempt to destroy human civilization.

Wives, mothers of families, the first educators of the human race in the intimacy of the family circle, pass on to your sons and your daughters the traditions of your elders at the same time that you prepare them for an unsearchable future. Always remember that by her children a mother belongs to that future which perhaps she will not see.

And you, women living alone, realize what you can accomplish through your dedicated vocation. Society is appealing to you on all sides. Not even families can live without the help of those who have no families. Especially you, consecrated virgins, in a world where egoism and the search for pleasure would become law, be the guardians of purity, unselfishness and piety. Jesus, who has given to conjugal love all its plenitudes, has also exalted the renouncement of human love when this is for the sake of divine love and for the service of all.

Lastly, women in trial, who stand upright at the foot of the cross like Mary, you who so often in history have given to humanity the strength to battle unto the very end and to give witness to the point of martyrdom, aid them now still once more to retain courage in their great undertakings, while at the same time maintaining patience and an esteem for humble beginnings.

Women, you do know how to make truth sweet, tender and accessible; make it your task to bring the spirit of this Council into institutions, schools, homes and daily life. Women of the entire universe, whether Christian or non-believing, you to whom life is entrusted at this grave moment in history, it is for you to save the peace of the world.

NOTE: This presentation was read by Leon Cardinal Duval of Algiers, Algeria, assisted by Julius Cardinal Doepfner of Munich, Germany, and Raul Cardinal Siloa of Santiago, Chile.

Message to the Poor, Sick and Suffering

To all of you, brothers and sisters in trial, who are visited by suffering under a thousand forms, the Council has a very special message. It feels in itself your pleading eyes, burning with fever or hollow with fatigue, questioning eyes which search in vain for the why of human suffering and which ask anxiously when and whence will come relief.

Very dear brethren, we feel echoing deeply within our hearts as fathers and pastors your laments and your complaints. Our suffering is increased at the thought that it is not within our power to bring you bodily help nor the lessening of your physical sufferings, which physicians, nurses and all those dedicated to the service of the sick are endeavoring to relieve as best they can.

But we have something deeper and more valuable to give you, the only truth capable of answering the mystery of suffering and of bringing you relief without illusion, and that is faith and union with the Man of Sorrows, with Christ the Son of God, nailed to the cross for our sins and for our salvation. Christ did not do away with suffering. He did not even wish to unveil to us entirely the mystery of suffering. He took suffering upon Himself and this is enough to make you understand all its value. All of you who feel heavily the weight of the cross, you who are poor and abandoned, you who weep, you who are persecuted for justice, you who are ignored, you the unknown victims of suffering, take courage. You are the preferred children of the kingdom of God, the kingdom of hope, happiness and life. You are the brethren of the suffering Christ, and with Him, if you wish, you are saving the world.

This is the Christian science of suffering, the only one which gives peace. Know that you are not alone, separated, abandoned or useless. You have been called by Christ and are His living and transparent image. In His name, the Council salutes you lovingly, thanks you, assures you of the friendship and assistance of the Church, and blesses you.

NOTE: This message was read by Paul Cardinal Meouchi, Maronite-Rite Patriarch of Antioch; assisted by Stefan Cardinal Wyszynski of Warsaw and Peter Cardinal Doi of Tokyo.

Message to Workers

In the course of this Council, we, the Catholic bishops of the five continents, have, among many other subjects, reflected together on the grave questions posed for human conscience by the economic and social conditions of the contemporary world, the coexistence of nations, the problem of armaments, of war and peace. We are fully aware of the repercussions which the solution provided for these problems can have on the concrete life of the working men and women of the entire world. Thus, at the end of our deliberations, we wish to address to all of them a message of confidence, peace and friendship.

Very loved sons and daughters, rest assured first of all that the Church is aware of your sufferings, your struggles and your hopes, and that she appreciates highly the virtues which ennoble your souls—namely courage, dedication, professional conscience, love of justice—and that she recognizes fully the immense services which, each in one's own place and in positions often the most obscure and the most ignored, you render to the whole of society. The Church is grateful to you for this and thanks you through our voice.

In these recent years, she has never ceased to keep before her eyes the increasingly complex problems of the working world; and, the echo which recent pontifical encyclicals have found in your ranks has proved to what degree the soul of workers of our time was attuned to that of the highest spiritual leaders. Pope John XXIII who enriched the patrimony of the Church with his incomparable messages knew how to find the road to your heart. He, in his own person, gave a shining example of the Church's love for working people as well as for truth, justice, liberty and charity, on which is founded the peace of the world. We wish also to be before you witnesses of this love of the Church for you workers, and we declare to you with all the conviction of our souls: The Church is your friend. Have confidence in her. In the past, regrettable misunderstandings have, over too long a period, maintained a spirit of mistrust and a lack of understanding between us, and both the Church and the working class have suffered from this. Today the hour for reconciliation has sounded and the Church of the Council invites you to celebrate this hour without suspicion.

The Church is ever seeking to understand you better. But on your part you must endeavor to understand what the Church means for you, workers, who are the chief artisans of the prodigious changes which the world is undergoing today. For you know full well that unless a mighty spiritual inspiration animates these changes, they will cause disaster for humanity instead of bringing it happiness. It is not hatred which serves the world. It is not only the bread of this earth which can satisfy human hunger. Thus, accept the message of the Church. Accept the faith which she offers you to light your path. It is the faith of the successor of Peter and of the 2,000 bishops assembled in Council. It is the faith of the Christian people. May it be your light. May it be your guide. May it bring you to the knowledge of Jesus Christ, your Companion in work, Master and Savior of the whole human race.

NOTE: This statement was read by Paul Cardinal Zoungrana of Ouagadougou, Upper Volta, assisted by Jose Cardinal Quintero of Caracas, Venezuela, and Jose Cardinal Bueno y Monreale of Seville, Spain.

Message to the Youth

Finally, it is to you, young men and women of the world, that the Council wishes to address its final message. For it is you who are to receive the torch from the hands of your elders and to live in the world at the period of the most gigantic transformations ever realized in its history. It is you who, receiving the best of the example of the teaching of your parents and your teachers, are to form the society of tomorrow. You will either save yourselves or you will perish with it.

For four years the Church has been working to rejuvenate her image in order to respond better to the design of her Founder, the great Living One, the Christ who is eternally young. At the end of this imposing re-examination of life, she now turns to you. It is for you youth, especially for you, that the Church now comes through her Council to enkindle your light, the light which illuminates the future, your future. The Church is anxious that this society that you are going to build up should respect the dignity, the liberty and the rights of individuals. These individuals are you. The Church is particularly anxious that this society should allow free expansion to her treasure ever ancient and ever new, namely faith, and that your souls may be able to bask freely in its helpful light. She has confidence that you will find such strength and such joy that you will not be tempted, as were some of your elders, to yield to the seductions of egoistic or hedonistic philosophies or to those of despair and annihilation; and, that in the face of atheism, a phenomenon of lassitude and old age, you will know how to affirm your faith in life and in what gives meaning to life, that is to say, the certitude of the existence of a just and good God.

It is in the name of this God and of His Son, Jesus, that we exhort you to open your hearts to the dimensions of the world, to heed the appeal of your brothers and sisters, to place your youthful energies at their service. Fight against all egoism. Refuse to give free reign to the instincts of violence and hatred which beget wars and all their train of miseries. Be generous, pure, respectful and sincere, and build in enthusiasm a better world than your elders had.

The Church looks to you with confidence and with love. Rich with a long past ever living in her, and marching on toward human perfection in time and the ultimate destinies of history and of life, the Church is the real youth of the world. She possesses what constitutes the strength and the charm of youth, that is to say, the ability to rejoice with what is beginning, to give oneself unreservedly, to renew one's self, and to set out again for new conquests. Look upon the Church and you will find in her the face of Christ, the genuine, humble and wise hero, the prophet of truth and love, the companion and friend of youth. It is in the name of Christ that we salute you, that we exhort and bless you.

NOTE: This address was read by Gregorio Cardinal Agagianian of the Roman Curia, assisted by Joseph Cardinal Ritter of Saint Louis, USA and Valerian Cardinal Gracias of Bombay, India.

9

APOSTOLIC BRIEF OF POPE PAUL VI CLOSING THE COUNCIL

The Second Vatican Ecumenical Council, assembled in the Holy Spirit and under the protection of the Blessed Virgin Mary, whom we have declared Mother of the Church, and of Saint Joseph, her glorious spouse, and of the Apostles Saints Peter and Paul, must be numbered without doubt among the greatest events of the Church. In fact, it was the largest in the number of Fathers who came to the seat of Peter from every part of the world, even from those places where the hierarchy has been very recently established. It was the richest because of the questions which for four sessions have been discussed carefully and profoundly. And last of all, it was the most opportune, because, bearing in mind the necessities of the present day, above all, it sought to meet the pastoral needs and, nourishing the flame of charity, it has made a great effort to reach not only the Christians still separated from communion with the Holy See, but also the whole human family.

At last, all which regards the holy Ecumenical Council has, with the help of God, been accomplished and all the constitutions, decrees, declarations and votes have been approved by the deliberation of the synod and promulgated by us. Therefore, we decided to close for all intents and purposes, with our apostolic authority, this same Ecumenical Council called by our predecessor, Pope John XXIII, which opened October 11, 1962, and which was continued by us after his death.

We decided, moreover, that all that has been established synodally is to be religiously observed by all the faithful, for the glory of God and the dignity of the Church and for the tranquility and peace of all people. We have approved and established these things, decreeing that the present letters are and remain stable and valid, and are to have legal effectiveness, so that they be disseminated and obtain full and complete effect, and so that they may be fully convalidated by those whom they concern or may concern now and in the future; and so that, as it be judged and described, all efforts contrary to these things by whomever or whatever authority, knowingly or in ignorance, be invalid and worthless from now on.

NOTE: This document *In Spiritu Sancto* was read at the closing ceremonies of Vatican II on December 8, 1965 by Archbishop Pericle Felici, general secretary of the Council. Pope Paul VI included in the document these final words: *Given in Rome at Saint Peter's, under the [seal of the] ring of the fisherman, December 8, on the feast of the Immaculate Conception of the Blessed Virgin Mary, the year 1965, the third year of our pontificate.*

10

THE CHURCH IN ASIA TWENTY AND FORTY YEARS AFTER VATICAN II
Personal Reflections: 1985 and 2005

Francisco F. Claver, S.J.

Introduction. Twenty years in the life of an institution is only a drop in the bucket—especially if the institutional bucket partakes somewhat of the attribute of eternity. Thus, to try assessing what has happened to the Catholic Church since the close of Vatican II in 1965 would probably be like attempting to trace a particular drop in a pailful of water to see what effect it has had on the other millions of drops in the bucket. It is an impossibility. But possibly, the image to use should be something else: a chemical reaction perhaps, leaven in the dough, an electrical charge to a dead battery—something more dynamic, something more life-giving. Considered this way, the little drop of water that Vatican II may seem to be will not be as innocent after all, even when looked at "with the eyes of eternity." For the incontrovertible fact is the Council has wrought change, great change, in the eternal Church of Christ, brief as the time has been since its ending twenty years ago.

Assessing the Change. This paper does not pretend to be a scientific study by any means. I write as a pastor—a former one, at any rate—whose active priesthood has coincided with the post-conciliar years. To all intents and purposes, that priesthood, from its very beginning, has been a never ending grappling with the Council's ideas.

"Grappling with ideas"—this probably is as good a summary as any of what has transpired these past twenty years for many of us. For Vatican II was essentially an idea—or ideas. *Aggiornamento*, opening to the modern world, reform, etc.—however one wants to describe what Pope John XXIII set out to do—the original idea has, in the course of the Council and in its aftermath, generated one rich idea after another, not always in an orderly way nor in clear logical sequence, but still conjoined in tight linkage one to another. It is this fact that makes for the great clarity and as well, paradoxically, for the just as great confusion that have marked the post-conciliar Church. The clarity-confusion phenomenon can be explained in other ways, of course, and the suspicion that the attitude of acceptance or non-acceptance with which people regard the Council even before they give serious consideration to its ideas may be for many *the* sole reason!

The grappling, at least for those in pastoral work who have taken the Council seriously, has not been in only speculating about the meaning and implications of the Council's ideas but also in working them out in actual pastoral practice. The most sterile speculation can become prolifically fruitful when the logic of ideas is worked out in practice. Nor has it been done in a solipsistic way, by one's individual efforts alone, but with others, with entire apostolic communities ranging all the way from base communities to dioceses, even whole regions. Again, it is amazing how communal thinking and acting become not only quantitatively but also qualitatively different from individual thinking and acting. The grappling, when done in active praxis and in community, is strangely not merely a summation of what Vatican II is all about; it also brings about a Vatican II Church.

It is for this reason then that we pursue the assessing of the impact of Vatican II on the Asian Church in the way we propose here. We are not going to ask what objectively the main idea or ideas of Vatican II is or are; nor what Asian theologians have done by way of advancing those ideas, developing them, enriching them; nor what pronouncements bishops and conferences of bishops, the entire FABC for that matter, have made relative to the initiatives of the Council. I do not doubt that the assessment we seek can be done by these and other unnamed means. The approach I propose to follow is rather simple and it is centered on these two questions: (1) What *single* Vatican II idea has led to the most radical change in the Church's pastoral work? And, (2) How does the Church of Asia measure up to that *one* idea?

Without doubt, many reasons—and good ones—can be adduced against the choice of those two questions and the manner of proceeding that they imply. But I propose them here, at least initially, as merely heuristic questions, as a springboard which, I hope, will launch further questions, lead to new answers.

The Key Pastoral Idea. If I were to choose among the many rich ideas of Vatican II, and, as was explicitly indicated above, from a *pastoral* point of view, I would not hesitate to put my finger on *participation.* Hence, I would define the most creative and effective pastoral initiatives arising from Vatican II in terms of the building up of a *more participatory Church.* One major idea among many? Or *the* key idea on which all the others depend? It probably does not matter how one answers these questions as long as these ideas do not remain merely on the conceptual level but are made to bear in practical ways on the life of the Church. For only in the latter context will their close interconnectedness be seen most clearly and in living fashion; and in this context it will not matter much either where one starts or what one believes is key. Inculturation, collegiality, co-responsibility, liturgical renewal, a theologically updated church, dialogue, etc.—these and many others of Council provenience will lead, by a logic of their own, to one another.

If the idea of participation is then taken as a summation of Vatican II, it is from a pastoral bias which looks always to what actually happens to people because of ideas or events or the action of other people. Hence the question: What happens when the Institutional Church begins to participate more fully in the life of people and—the other side of the same coin—when the people likewise begin to participate just as fully in the life of the Church? Many things happen—and quite inevitably. Five very obvious effects are noted here.

(1) A Change of Focus. When the ethic of participation takes hold of a Church community, there is a shift of focus from hierarchical leadership to lay follower-ship, from the institution to its membership, from canonical concerns to the life problems of the people. It is not that hierarchy, institution and ecclesiastical law are no longer of consequence. They still are. But like the Sabbath, they are put in the perspective they are meant to be in: at the service of people—not the other way around. It is this "paradigm shift," more than any other it seems, that has brought about the biggest change in the Church these past twenty years. It is also the most recalcitrant of change where the old order is most entrenched and the change is interpreted more in terms of power than of service. The logic of the change resulting from the shift is simply that when people—the laity, whose role in Church society vis-à-vis hierarchical and clerical leadership has for long been defined in terms of a client-patron relationship—are asked to participate more fully in the life of the Church and begin to take their rightful place in that same Church, narrow visions get broadened and, as well, the scope of the activities of the laity as participants in the evangelizing mission of the Church.

(2) Social Transformation. The shift just noted above leads to another: the acceptance of the transforming power of the Gospel not just for individuals but for communities and societies as a whole. Conversion, in other words, is seen to have personal as well as social dimensions. Again, the logic flows from the archetypal idea of participation. When the rank-and-file members of the Church are brought fully into the evangelizing task of the Church, to participate actively in the task, they see at once that the Gospel is not meant only for that sphere of life that is called spiritual; it is for the whole of life—for the spiritual and the moral, yes, but also for the political, the economic, the cultural, the social, etc. And the Gospel must be made to bear on these other spheres, to transform them, change them for the better, sublimate them, so that in truth the whole of life becomes truly Christian. The task is seen both as a personal mission and as a communal one. Not just the individual Christian but the whole community of believers must work towards the transforming of themselves and the world around them into the Kingdom of Christ.

(3) Discernment. The task of the Church thus understood is not going to be done without plenty of thinking and consulting preceding it and accompanying it at every step. Everyone in the community has something to contribute to the task. But what that contribution is, how it is to be made, these cannot be answered except in a continuous analytical and reflecting process engaged in by both the individual and the whole community, and beyond analysis and reflection, prayerful discernment from faith. We can not put too much stress on the discerning-from-faith character of a participative Church in regard to its task and on the centrality of faith values as the ultimate criteria in its discernment. Failing these, as experience from the field shows time and again, the faith-community becomes merely a sociological entity, its discernment purely an "analysis of the situation," its criteria of judging and evaluating events dictated mainly by ideological and political considerations. The participants in the discerning process are first and foremost men and women of faith and their discerning is hence a conscious striving to read the signs of the times with and in the Spirit of Christ. A Spirit-filled Church—but a deeply involved one—will be the immediate result of the kind of discernment we speak of here.

(4) Inculturation. A quite significant development in most Third World Churches, one that has stemmed and evolved from Council ideas about reform and renewal, is a strong pre-occupation with inculturation—the effort to express and live the faith in terms and ways more attuned to the symbols and traditions of a people. In places where the movement towards the development of a more participative Church is strong, the inculturative process is also far advanced. The strong correlation of the two is not hard to see. When people are allowed to participate more fully in the life of the Church as active members, they will do so *as themselves*, i.e., as bearers of a particular culture. This means they will bring into their participation ways of thinking and doing that are part of their cultural heritage, express and do the faith along lines more in keeping with their cultural tradition. This was not always so in the past when the thinking and doing part in the Church was practically the monopoly of Church leaders trained in Western cultural traditions. In the inculturative process, the solidest of foundations are laid for the creation of truly local Churches.

(5) A New Way of Being Church. The idea of a local Church—the Church not only *in* but also *of* a place and people—is a new one, for our generation at least. The Church becomes local, practically inevitably, again for the sole reason that when people begin participating in its life, they bring into its ambit of concern their own life concerns. This has the effect of both broadening and narrowing the Church's pastoral outlook: broadening it, that is, beyond its explicitly spiritual concerns;

narrowing it to the specificities of the people's life as they see it and as they try to live it in a Christian way as *this* people and not as generalized Christians. What eventually happens in a truly participatory and discerning Church, given the change of focus and the acceptance of social transformation and inculturation as legitimate tasks in the over-all mission of the Church, is a new way of being Church. From the simple idea of participation, questions about the nature of the Church arise which would otherwise not have been asked before except by professional theologians. And from questions of an ecclesiological nature, further ones are proposed about spiritualities—what Gospel values to stress in the new thrust, how to work them into a comprehensive whole to give Christians direction in their work *as* Church. All these questions about ecclesiologies and spiritualities are in turn thrown back to the people to reflect on, discuss, develop, improve, in a process of participative discernment.

In 1982, at the FABC General Assembly, this new way of being Church was talked about in terms of the Church as Communion. Whatever theologians say about this particular model of the Church, viewed from a pastoral point of view and brought down to specific pastoral programs, it will come down to what we call a participatory Church. The distinctive note of such a Church, one soon realizes, is *sharing*—and sharing is but another name for charity, the essential message of Christ's Gospel and the effective bond of unity in a Church of Communion. A Church that is fully participatory is thus a most powerful and living sacrament of Christian charity in act.

Strategy of Change. The choice of participation as the key idea of Vatican II is dictated not by good pastoral practice alone but by equally good social science as well—at least that branch of it that deals with change in society. Social change is a complex phenomenon, but to simplify it a bit, there are two general aspects of society that change agents ordinarily pay careful attention to in their efforts to bring about holistic change: cultural values and social structures. These two are supportive of each other, and theoretically, a change in one will bring about change in the other, and to the extent that they supplement and support each other, the resulting change will not be too disruptive of society—yet for all that can be as radical as any brought about by more revolutionary methods.

Looking at the creation of a more participatory Church as a phenomenon of social change within the Church, we cannot but note its validity precisely as a process of change. When participation and its germane values (social transformation, co-responsibility, dialogue, communal discernment, human dignity, the moral power of acting believers, etc.) are effectively interiorized, they will result in a radical restructuring of the social fabric of the Church. Similarly, when structures of participation (base communities, parish councils, pastoral councils, synods, etc.) become operative as ordinary parts of the institutional Church, they will reinforce the new values that are connoted by the term "participatory Church."

In fine, the plethora of ideas offered by Vatican II— revolutionary and dynamic ideas all, whether taken singly or collectively—will be largely ineffective except in the full acceptance of the basic idea of participation. This conclusion might seem to be too sweeping and hence as invalid as any other broad generalization. But it is based on the general principle—and it falls or stands on the validity of this principle— that socio-cultural change (change involving whole peoples) will not catch unless it is understood, decided on, acted on, in a word, *participated in*, by as wide a spectrum as possible of the members of the society undergoing change. It is for this reason that the notion—and practice—of an ever more and more participatory Church is felt to be *the* most revolutionary idea coming from Vatican II and hence the yardstick to use in assessing developments—anywhere—in the post-conciliar Church. I would like to use this yardstick in this little effort to make sense out of the Asian Church today.

The Church of Asia. In so far as it is possible to conceive of it as an entity, the Church of Asia is not just a bucket of water but a whole ocean. To say something about it then beyond unhelpful generalities would not be worth attempting except for this one specific fact that the one dominant model of the Church throughout the continent prior to Vatican II (as it was throughout the world) was that of the Institutional Church. There is hence a common starting ground from which to assess it. If participation is thus used as the standard of measurement, it is possible to say something at least about the temperature of the water of the vast ocean that is the Church of Asia. From this standpoint, three areas of assessment—impressionistic for the most part, true, but still not devoid entirely of validity—present themselves for consideration: the extent of acceptance of the participatory model; lay leadership; and obstacles to change.

(1) The Extent of Participation. The best criterion for judging to what extent the ethic of participation has caught in any Church is to see whether and how far the concept of the BEC— the basic ecclesial community—has been accepted in pastoral practice. If the BEC is used here as the measure of change, it is because participation at all levels and in all areas of community life is of the essence of the BEC. This contrasts sharply with the traditional parish which is by definition hierarchical in structure and function and rather minimalist as far as lay participation is concerned. The two—the BEC and the traditional parish— represent hence two kinds of Churches and provide us with ideal types for comparative purposes.

The traditional parish and all it stands for is still the modal form of Church throughout Asia. If ideas and practices of Vatican II have been incorporated into it, their over-all effect does not seem to have had too great an impact on old outlooks and structures of the Church. All too often, for instance, lay ministers, if they are accepted, tend to be clericalized lay men; pastoral councils, where they exist, are rigidly run as consultative bodies (which, it must be said, is what Canon Law says they are), the possibility of their evolving into fully deliberative bodies actively discouraged; lay associations are of the "mandated organization" type, concerned mostly with "churchy" interests; and "spiritual" movements like the *cursillo* and charismatic renewal groups are geared mainly towards personal sanctification.

The BEC kind of Church is, however, slowly gaining ground. There is genuine interest shown it in many countries of the continent and in some its development is quite advanced. True, the BEC admits of many definitions depending on the kind and extent of participation it accords the laity. In its most basic form, it is mainly a liturgical community in which active lay participation is seen not as only a concession to the laity but as their full right—though its interests still tend to be personal conversion and sanctification. In other forms of the BEC, the social implications of the Gospel are given as much attention as personal spiritual growth and holiness, and the community's worship and pastoral programs reflect this wider vision of the Church and its mission. It is in these latter types of BECs too that genuine discernment and inculturation are taking place with more than a modicum of success.

From a merely quantitative angle, the development of BECs in Asia has barely gotten off the ground, but to judge from what seems to be a burgeoning groundswell of interest in them in practically every country of Asia, the prognosis is most hopeful. If the growing interest means anything, it is that the idea of a participative Church is at least in principle rather widely accepted and everywhere the search is on for a vehicle for its promotion. This judgment is bolstered by the latest development—an interest in lay leadership formation.

(2) Lay Leadership. The newest instrument of the FABC to be created is the FABC "Office for the Laity." So far it has centered on lay leadership formation and has already held the first three planned regional institutes on lay leadership. What is of significance to us here is not so much the institutes themselves and their effectivity as the simple fact of the Committee's creation and its focus on leadership. For, as has already been noted above, it does bespeak a movement that is gaining strength and its whole direction is towards empowering the laity and getting them to participate more actively in the Church's task of evangelization.

If at this time the concentration of efforts is on the formation of lay leaders, it is so in the understanding, unspoken but real nonetheless, of the fact that participative communities cannot be fostered without a participative leadership. A new kind of leadership in the Church, in other words, or perhaps better, a new way of exercising leadership (not only by lay people but by clergy and hierarchy as well) is being consciously created and it is geared towards encouraging participation in the Church by the rank and file of Christians beyond merely attending church and giving financial support for its pastoral programs. The fact is well understood in such dioceses and parishes as have made the formation of BEC types of communities an express target in their pastoral priorities, and their experience in this regard is beginning to be more widely consulted. Already in not a few dioceses, there is a growing sense that the notion of lay leader is not exhausted by, nor co-terminous with, the notion of lay minister. The latter's concern is with liturgical matters—the dispensation of the sacraments, the conduct of worship, the preaching of the Word; the former's goes beyond into other areas of Christian community living—economic development, social justice, communal action on problems of consequence for the good of society at large, the integration of faith *and* life. But in this as in other aspects of change and renewal in the Church's life, there are obstacles of no little moment to overcome.

(3)   Obstacles to Change.   I am not too sure that the obstacles to the creation of more participative Churches are any different in Asia than in the rest of the world—except perhaps for some facts of a cultural nature that may be distinctive of Asian peoples.   The one biggest hindrance has already been alluded to: the deeply entrenched concept of the Church as Institution (and this in its Western form).   It is for all practical purposes the only model of Church that we know and for all its virtues, it is not *the* model that one should foster if one is interested in developing a Church that will encourage lay participation to the fullest extent and allow for its widest exercise within its own internal structuring.   If, as was noted early on, holistic change entails attending to both the values and the social structuring of a society to ensure their mutual reinforcement in the process of change, integral change without too much conflict will be very difficult where the values and the structures of the older order · are firmly in possession and there is strong resistance to any threat or danger to their continuance.

The difficulty is compounded when, as in Asia, traditional respect for elders is transferred to ecclesiastical leaders and the ethic of participation is interpreted as an erosion of their authority and power.

These difficulties are very real and it would be most unrealistic to believe that they can be overcome overnight.   But there is hope in the fact that all over Asia today there is a stirring— approaching unease—towards thoughts and preoccupations which were not there before Vatican II and which are centered precisely on the concept of a more participatory Church. If the discernment on these and germane ideas continues and is carried on by ever wider segments of the Church's membership, that very discerning is the beginning of the participative kind of Church that we have in effect been equating with a Vatican II Church.

Conclusion. There is a lot more to be said, certainly, about the Church of Asia and the changes that have—or have not—taken place in the wake of Vatican II. We have not gone into such factors as the great diversity and strength of cultures in Asia, of the Great Traditions especially and their—to date—impermeability to Christianity; the minority status of the Church in most Asian countries and what the fact means for the more visible presence of the Church that Vatican II seems to ask for; the many initiatives taken by the FABC through its various instrumentalities and their impact on the Church in general; and on a very particular level, such Asia-wide institutions (like the East Asian Pastoral Institute) and their contributions to the general level of renewal in the Asian Church. But crucial as these and many more factors may be, their importance can only be guessed at here. Their proper evaluation and the action taken from their evaluation have to be done on the level of each local Church. It is to that level the responsibility belongs.

This last statement is not as jejune as it seems. For by making participation the standard by which to judge what has happened in the Churches of Asia as a result of Vatican II, we have in a very real sense been asking how capable are they for self-appraisal and self-regulation for the changes that Vatican II represents, what mechanisms have they created for common discernment and action, what real efforts have they expended and are still expending towards these ends.

Still, even without fully researched answers to these questions, one cannot help concluding that there is a vitality to the Churches of Asia that is quite readily apparent; and the vitality is there because the participatory ethic of Vatican II is beginning to take [published in October 1985].

Retrospective. The above was written twenty years ago in 1985. Rereading it another twenty years later—forty years, all told, after Vatican II—I come to the conclusion it still is right on target in what it says about the efforts in the Church of Asia to become a truly participatory Church. Those efforts have in fact redoubled and strengthened in most places. Three events or developments bolster my conclusion: the first is local, the PCP II (the Second Plenary Council of the Philippines) in 1991; the second is Asia-wide, the Asian Synod of 1998; and joining the two is the common acceptance of the AsIPA—the Asian Integral Pastoral Approach—in all the Churches of Asia. A brief word about each of these three.

(1) The Second Plenary Council of the Philippines (PCP II). The PCP II was held in Manila January 20 to February 18, 1991 (the first ever that was conducted according to the revised canons governing plenary councils). Its main thrust was the renewal of the Philippine Church—and renewal to be worked at as precisely *the* Local Church of the Philippines. A major pastoral priority decided on by the Council concerned the basic ecclesial community. When one considers the thrust of its final document and the wealth of resolutions it approved, the conclusion is not hard to come by that the Council's full implementation can be done mostly and best in the BECs and in fact will lead to their formation (where they have not yet been started) and to their strengthening (where they are already existing). In a very real sense then, the PCP II was the

Philippine Church's official *reception* of Vatican II. It is specific to the Philippines, but in the interchange that takes place at the FABC level, at the level of its joint commissions especially, the experience of each country does have a hearing among and an influence on the other Churches of Asia. If the BEC is indeed the focus and vehicle of renewal, a participatory community *par excellence,* its choice as a top pastoral priority by the Plenary Council only means that the Philippine Church as a whole has embraced fully the participatory Church ideal as something to strive for.

(2)　**The Asian Synod.** The special Synod for Asia was held in Rome April 18 to May 16, 1998. The bishop delegates from the countries comprising the FABC were quite united and forceful in pushing for ideas that the Federation had been concerned with over the years—the triple dialogue especially with cultures, religions and the poor. The triple dialogue had been continually discerned on in assemblies of the Federation, advocated strongly by the FABC from its very inception as a Federation in Manila in 1970. It has in its concept and practice carried implications official Rome was not always comfortable with, but it was pushed strongly nonetheless at the Synod. Ideas tightly related to dialogue—inculturation, the Local Church, social justice, etc.—all were talked about at length and reiterated again and again as concerns to be worked at by all the Churches of Asia. Their repetitive and variant ways of expressing these concerns helped modify somewhat Rome's constant reminder that the explicit preaching of Christ had to be made in order for true evangelization to occur. The Asian bishops quietly insisted that the example of silent witnessing to Gospel values was as valid a way of evangelizing as the explicit kind—in some situations on the continent, the *only* way. In that insistence the bishops were simply being faithful to what the Council had taught about the dialogue the Church must enter into with people and their world, a dialogue which cannot be carried out authentically except in the context of a participatory Church. And the model of such a Church was again and again that of grass-roots communities like the BECs.

(3) **The AsIPA.** If there is anything that has developed strongly among the Churches of Asia in recent years which solidifies their acceptance of the triple dialogue with cultures, religions and the poor, and hence the development of a more participatory Church, it would be, to my mind, the AsIPA—the Asian Integral Pastoral Approach—and its rather wide acceptance, at least among FABC member Churches.   A methodology of evangelization, one might call it. Its main components are discernment on life problems and situations based on prayer and reflection, on scripture and planned action on the fruits of discernment in a continuous cycle of discerning and acting from faith by a whole community. The methodology is actually that of the BECs—and indeed a methodology that would bring about the formation and development of BEC-type communities. There is nothing specifically Asian about it except that it has been appropriated by the Churches of Asia—or at least by various pastoral workers in them—as their own way of evangelizing. The methodology requires participation by all members of a Church community. It is, hence, by its very nature, dialogic: first among members themselves, then with others not of the faith but to whom their action is extended, but above all with the Spirit in the discernment process that is an essential part of their activity and being as Church. The methodology requires a strong social involvement by the community.   But most importantly, it develops a spirituality of discernment that depends heavily on prayer based on Scripture. What this all means is that the Church of Asia, by its adoption of the AsIPA as its pastoral methodology, is becoming a Church more and more according to the image of an authentic Vatican II Church.

Conclusion. The point of view I assumed in the 1985 article reproduced above was unabashedly impressionistic. In the twenty years since it was written, the impressionistic to my mind has become more and more *the* real. The direction set by the FABC from the very beginning of its existence is still the direction its member Churches are striving faithfully to follow. That fact compels strongly to this conclusion: The Church of Asia, despite its many defects and problems, is a Church that has wholeheartedly embraced and made its own the renewing and reforming thrust of Vatican II. Its continuing efforts at becoming such a Church make for a vibrant life, committed, hope-filled [August 22, 2005]. [NOTE: This text was received in late 2005; sincere gratitude is expressed to the author for his contribution. – Editor]

11

CONSECRATED LIFE IN ASIA FORTY YEARS AFTER VATICAN II
Reality and Challenges

Julma C. Neo, D.C.

Introduction. Any attempt to reflect on consecrated life in Asia after Vatican II must necessarily start from an awareness of developments in the continent and in the Churches of Asia within the past several decades. Consecrated life is in the Church and it is always profoundly affected by changes in it. These latter are in turn responses to developments in society and in the world. Consecrated life, the Church and the world are inseparable realities.

Asia: A Continent of Many Faces. Taking a close look at the continent shortly after Vatican II, the Federation of Asian Bishops' Conferences (FABC) remarked that Asia wears many faces. It is the face of teeming millions comprising about two-thirds of the world's population of nearly six billion, many of whom are young. It is the face of millions of poor living in poverty and in misery side by side with islands of great affluence in many countries. It is the face of great religious and cultural diversity. Asia is home to 85% of the adherents of the world's great non-Christian religions as well as other religious traditions. It is likewise the cradle of several ancient civilizations that antedate Christianity.

During the past few decades, this Asian face has been undergoing rapid and dramatic changes that are altering its profile and transforming the lives of its people. In some ways, Asia reflects the great diversity and contrasts that one finds in the world: rapid development and underdevelopment, the traditional and the modern, the ancient and the new, mega-cities and villages, fast and slow societies (technologically speaking), democracies, monarchies, socialism, and governments in transition. One finds an ever widening gap between the rich and the poor within and among countries, social injustice, urbanization, modernization and globalization with their accompanying socio-cultural problems; human and environmental pollution and cultural dislocation have become permanent features of most Asian societies. Relatively peaceful societies contrast with those torn apart by conflicts and wars. Religious fundamentalism is on the rise in many countries, posing a threat on many levels—religious, social and political.

Clearly, Asia is a continent continually caught in a dynamic interplay between lights and shadows, life-giving and death-dealing forces, and always filled with challenges and expectations, life and hope.

Ecclesial Realities. The Church in Asia reflects the great diversity that characterizes the continent. Christians are present throughout the continent but in varying degrees. Most live in the midst of largely non-Christian milieus, except in the Philippines and East Timor whose populations are for the most part Christian. There are Churches living under restricted circumstances in socialist countries where religious persecution still exists. Other Churches live in a more stable political environment that allows greater freedom. A number of

Churches have to struggle under repressive or fundamentalist governments that are hostile to Christians. Some others are inserted in milieus that are very developed economically. A variety of Eastern Churches with their own rites are found in West and South Asia. There are Churches that are "centuries old" and others that are "newly born."

The Churches of Asia are at different stages with regard to the renewal launched by Vatican II. Renewal has been slow in some places due either to the lack of conciliar materials translated into the people's own language or because of resistance to change, in general. In other instances, particularly in countries under socialist regimes, political factors have made this renewal practically impossible until more recently. In still others, steps towards more organized forms of renewal have been taken more or less according to a pace set by the leadership in the local Churches.

Partly due to a colonial past and to the fact of continued financial support from abroad, the Church in many parts of Asia has an image of being a "foreign Church." Moreover, in the minds of many Asians, to be Christian is to be cut off from one's cultural roots and to lose one's national identity. This image remains very much a block to evangelization today (cf. IL:SA 13; EA 21).

The Church in Asia is a paradoxical Church. In one sense, it is a "little flock" at the margins that suffers from a "minority complex." In another sense, it enjoys considerable influence and reputation in many countries due to its institutional connections and access to human and material resources. This paradoxical reality has evoked mixed sentiments among its members and has sent ambivalent signals to those around them.

Since the early 1970s, the Federation of Asian Bishops'

Conferences (FABC) has continually reflected on these realities in the continent and has elaborated a vision of what the Church in Asia must become (FAPA III, pp. 3ff). If the Church in Asia has to be faithful to her mission, she must become a Church "incarnate in a people" and "inculturated" (FAPA I, p. 14). The 1998 Special Synod for Asia reiterated the imperative enunciated by the FABC in 1974 for the Church to engage in a triple dialogue: dialogue with Asian peoples, especially the poor, dialogue with their diverse cultures, and dialogue with their ancient religious traditions (cf. M:SA, 5).

In 1990, the FABC further articulated that the Church in Asia must be a "Servant Church" (cf. FAPA I, p. 283, 340), a "Church of the Poor" (FAPA I, p. 5) accompanying the Asian peoples in their search for fuller life. Mission for the Church in Asia means sharing through love and service the fullness of life that Jesus came to bring. The Churches in Asia must exemplify the communion that is at the heart of the Trinitarian life. The local Church is a communion of communities that must be in communion with other local Churches and with the See of Peter. All these imply a "new way of being Church" (FAPA I, p. 287).

It is this complex and continually evolving network of very diverse human and ecclesial realities that forms the context within which consecrated persons in Asia have tried to renew their life and mission according to the orientations of Vatican II during these past forty years.

Reality of Consecrated Life in Asia. Today there are over 180,000 consecrated women and men in Asia trying to live faithfully according to their founder's charism.[1] Of this number, 145,413 are women. Most are engaged in education, social

---

[1]Maximus Fernando, "Present Situation of Consecrated Life in Asia: A Sociological Approach," *Religious Life Asia* 6:1 (2004), 51-52.

work or health care in institutions. Ministries in these settings are generally well organized, very professional and of high standards according to the demands of contemporary times.[2] Oftentimes these institutions are among the best known in the country. Most Catholic schools can count among those who have crossed their portals, men and women from different religious beliefs who would later take on significant responsibilities in different fields of endeavor and thereby exercise considerable influence at different levels in their societies. Some religious involve themselves in pastoral work and in new forms of ministry among the poor. Institutes in socialist countries that are unable to run institutions now as they used to do in the past and have turned to pastoral work, social work and health care in non-institutional forms. More recently, however, some have begun to recover what they lost in the past (e.g. institutional works, properties). This new development and its impact on the life of the institute are posing new challenges to its members. All these varieties of ministries that are undertaken by consecrated women and men in Asia condition in many ways their lifestyle.

The diversity of the reality of consecrated life in the continent is likewise reflected in its membership. Institutes, particularly in some countries under socialist regimes, that have started to open up to the world, are experiencing a springtime. In a few very developed countries, there is a marked decline in membership and an increase in aging members. In many other Asian countries, consecrated life is generally stable and dynamic.

---

[2]These realities were verified by participants (bishops and major superiors of religious men and women from all over Asia) in the Symposium on Consecrated Life held in Thailand from July 20-22, 2005, sponsored by the FABC Office for Consecrated Life (FABC:OCL); see *FABC Papers 116*.

The years after Vatican II have shown that consecrated persons in Asia are in various stages of renewal depending, for the most part, on the extent of the renewal realized in the local Church itself, the political regime under which they live, their own exposure to external influences, opportunities for travel or studies outside the country and on the "congregational culture" that may be either closed or open to change. Many institutes can count among their members those that have been continually at the forefront of renewal in the local Church. In general, consecrated persons in Asia have been making significant contributions in furthering the mission of the Church.

A new development in the history of consecrated life in the continent is a growth in the number of those being sent on mission to other Asian countries, as well as to countries outside the continent. As part of the new geography of vocations in the universal Church today, many Asian religious[3] have assumed the leadership on the general level in international institutes even as the presence of Asian religious doing service in the West continues to grow. This Asian presence is transforming the face of many institutes in a more visible way and is making its impact more and more felt on the international scene.

Challenges. Forty years after Vatican II, one can say that consecrated life in Asia is not in crisis, as it is elsewhere. But it needs to undergo a real "face lifting," a visible alteration of its profile, as visible as the profound changes that are transforming Asian societies so that it could be perceived and seen in a new way by Asian peoples. "Seeing" impacts more powerfully on Asian peoples rather than "hearing." Images and symbols communicate meanings more eloquently. Given this Asian characteristic and contemporary challenges to consecrated life,

---

[3]In this article, consecrated persons and religious are used interchangeably, not in the strict sense of Canon Law.

presenting a "new face," a "new image" of consecrated persons that can resonate with the deep quest for fuller life among their fellow Asians constitutes a major challenge for consecrated persons in Asia. Such "image" or "face" must reflect very clearly *who* they claim to be. Asian peoples are longing to see this "new face" of consecrated persons. Even when they are not always able to articulate the object of their desire, they are continually searching for consecrated persons who will reflect to them the face of a *servant* who is both a *mystic* and a *prophet*. It is this face they will recognize as "Good News."

Servants. For consecrated persons to put on the face of a *servant,* they need to be in *solidarity* with millions of Asian peoples that are poor. For the past decades, solidarity has challenged consecrated persons in Asia to make their own "the joy and hope, the grief and anguish of the men of our time" (GS 1), to share the life of the poor, to live in physical and psychological proximity to them and to let their option for them influence their lives more significantly. It has motivated consecrated persons to commit themselves to working *with* the poor, to be their voice when they are voiceless and to help transform the societal structures that keep them in misery (FAPA I, pp. 15ff.). Solidarity has continually pushed consecrated persons in Asia towards "creative charity" (cf. NMI 50; SAC 33, 36), towards more determined and continued efforts to revise their life and works.

If one were to review the renewal efforts of institutes along this direction, one could see that signs of hope are not wanting. Revision of life and work among some institutes has resulted in greater simplicity of lifestyle and new forms of ministries that include not only assistance but also human promotion, advocacy, works for justice, peace and the integrity of creation. However, the number of those that have taken this direction has been a minority.

During the past few decades, some religious have started to re-read their charism through the optic of their option for the poor. There are small communities living and working among the very poor—sometimes in high-risk areas, imbued with a new vision of the poor that sees them as protagonists in their own development. They have taken on a new way of relating with the poor and those who collaborate with them, a way marked by equality and reciprocity. A number of institutes have re-directed some of their institutions towards ministries with the "new poor," victims of the economic order created by globalization. Others have adopted community-based ministries as an alternative to institutional ministries. Apostolic experiences among the poor are part of formation programs both for their members and for their lay collaborators. These signs of hope are a service that consecrated persons render Asian peoples.

However, obstacles have not been negligible. Given the institutional mentality and the middle class status that many consecrated persons in Asia have assumed, solidarity still remains a formidable challenge now and in the future. The insistence on professionalism and competence that is felt very strongly among religious in many parts of Asia today in the wake of globalization and modernization, particularly among those engaged in institutional ministries, has given consecrated persons a "specialist outlook" that has made it difficult for them to be simply in the midst of their people and to be present to their concerns. In many places, a rather inflexible lifestyle created or reinforced by imposing structures and material edifices that surround religious has made them irrelevant to their social context and inaccessible to people, particularly the poor. They project an image of being "islands of affluence" in the midst of "oceans of poverty."

To take on the face of a *servant* also implies for consecrated persons in Asia the promotion of *communion* within and outside their religious institutes in line with the orientations of Vatican II and other post Conciliar documents (cf. NMI 43; VC 46; SAC 28). A deep personal communion with the Trinity is an indispensable condition for this service of communion.   It provides the necessary foundation for building local communities where members are able to live unity in diversity and to collaborate among themselves and with others beyond their institutes and even beyond the Church (cf. VC 51-52; SAC 30-32).

Harmony is a core Asian value but its lack is evident in many Asian countries. Various forms of division exist (e.g. ethnic and religious, economic, political, socio-cultural and generational) (cf. IL:SA 39). Even Christian Churches have not been spared this reality. This constitutes a stumbling block to their witness to unity. These realities in the continent make the service of *communion* even more an imperative for consecrated persons in Asia.

In Asia, there are visible and more conscious efforts to promote communion by improving the quality of relationships and life in local communities; this means fostering greater participation of its members in all that concerns their life and mission and creating communities of reconciliation and healing, often in collaboration with those from different institutes and from other religions. On the national level, communion is fostered by inter-provincial and inter-congregational collaboration among institutes, among men and women religious, especially in the areas of ministry, formation and leadership. Many institutes are sharing their spirituality with the laity. On the continental level, communion is facilitated by structures such as the South East Asian Major Superiors Association (SEAMS), Asia-Pacific Meeting of Religious (AMOR), and the FABC Office for Consecrated Life (FABC:OCL). On the level of local Churches, there are mixed Commissions of bishops and major superiors functioning with varying degrees of effectiveness.

Efforts at communion in the local Church are, however, sometimes hindered by lack of a pastoral plan. In other cases, a lack of understanding of the various charisms in the Church contributes to these difficulties. The clerical, hierarchical and patriarchal mentality that characterizes many Asian cultures and the structures that embody them also make communion difficult in the concrete (cf. FAPA I, pp. 193-194). This mentality is reinforced at times by an exaggerated emphasis on some elements in traditional Asian cultures (e.g. excessive dependence on authority, too much deference to age, conformity to the group, etc.). With the "new culture" that is sweeping across Asian societies, the threat of individualism to families and religious communities has become very real. Some religious communities have become simply convenient "boarding houses" for "working religious." Team work is very difficult and a spirit of competitiveness has slowly crept in among some very professional religious. Multiculturalism and internationality in some Asian communities pose difficulties.

Dialogue, particularly with people from other religions, is another challenge for consecrated persons in Asia. Given the fact that, according to the *Pontifical Yearbook 2004,* only 17.2% of the world's population is Catholic, a future without interreligious dialogue is unthinkable. In Asia, where Christians are less than 3% of the population, this dialogue becomes even more urgent. Lessons from the history of evangelization in the continent reinforce this necessity.

If consecrated persons in Asia are to be "humble servants" of their people, dialogue must become a way of life for them and a permanent stance in all their relationships: interpersonal, intra-congregational, intra-ecclesial, societal, inter-cultural and interreligious. Such dialogue has to be grounded in the spirituality of the incarnation and of *kenosis.*

For the past decades, the Church in Asia has continually spoken of several levels of interreligious dialogue, i.e. dialogue of life, dialogue of action, dialogue of discourse, and dialogue of religious experience. Consecrated persons are very much engaged in these levels of dialogue in varying degrees. Most carry on the dialogue of life daily. Many undertake common action with women and men from different religions for the promotion of the poor and of women, for works of justice and peace and the integrity of creation. In some places, they share prayer and God experiences with their brothers and sisters from other religions and religious traditions as well as from other Christian denominations. There is an increasing number of centers for joint theological reflection and interfaith studies run by religious institutes. Studies of other religions form part of the formation programs of some institutes.

There are, however, many blocks to dialogue that still need to be overcome (e.g. fears, insecurities, suspicion of proselytizing from hostile governments, prejudices, complexes and a negative religious-political environment). Previous experiences of dialogue that are negative or unsuccessful constitute other hindrances. Dialogue is possible only when there is a felt sense of equality and respect among the partners in dialogue. Prevailing social structures in Asian societies and a hierarchical/patriarchal mentality that significantly impacts many Asian cultures often add to this difficulty in the concrete. Inadequate knowledge, poor interpersonal relationships, and lack of preparation (e.g. not having the needed skills), make religious ill prepared for dialogue, particularly interreligious dialogue.

Mystics. In Asia, the credibility of religious leaders of different religions rests on moral authority that is a fruit of their religious experience (cf. IL:SA 23). Becoming men and women of God, joyful spiritual persons, "icons of holiness," saintly persons that "show" the way rather than "speak" about it forms another major challenge for consecrated persons in Asia. Asian peoples want "humble, happy and prayerful religious rather than just achievers, specialists or professionals."[4] Asians are searching for *mystics* who can help them find God, primarily because they themselves have encountered Him. This challenge resonates well with the injunction of Vatican II that religious strive for holiness as they, together with the entire Church, have a vocation to holiness (cf. LG 39-42).

A spirituality that reflects a deep passion for Christ and compassion for their suffering brothers and sisters must characterize Asian religious if they are to make a difference in the continent. This spirituality must be born of their radical following of Christ who is God and at the same time incarnate, who made himself brother and servant to all, who preached the Good News that liberates people from whatever oppresses and hinders them from fullness of life. It needs to be rooted in the experience of Christ with special emphasis on compassion and harmony, detachment and self-emptying and be continually nourished by contemplating His face in prayer, in Scripture, in the Eucharist as well as in the faces of wounded humanity. This kind of spirituality will impel consecrated persons towards solidarity with the poor and will also lead them to dialogue with the Spirit present in the "signs of the times" and in the "seeds of the Word" in the various religions and cultures of Asia.

Today, a continuing renewal among consecrated persons in a spirituality that is truly evangelical, ecclesial, missionary, integral and Asian (because it draws from the spiritual resources already present among the people—in their cultures and in their

---

[4]Unpublished manuscript *Report of the Bishops' Conferences and Religious in Asia* presented at the Pre-Synodal Consultation on Religious Life held in Thailand, May 1994.

religious traditions) is a sign of hope in the continent. Throughout Asia, there are centers for spirituality run by religious institutes that continually offer opportunities for spiritual renewal for religious, lay and clergy.

The efforts towards renewal in spirituality, however, have not been without difficulties. A kind of religiosity that lays much emphasis on external devotions and observances can prove inadequate in the face of challenges posed by today's world. This inadequacy also shows itself in a lack of depth and commitment to the exigencies of consecrated life. Sometimes this may be the result of a faith nurtured in a traditional setting whose elements have not been integrated in the spirituality of the religious. This seems to be the case of religious coming from traditional cultures that join institutes that have been influenced by modern or western cultures and who have been unable to arrive at a harmonious integration of both cultures. This lack of spiritual integration—and its resulting syncretism, in some cases—provides a weak foundation when religious have to cope with the challenges of modernity that presently confront them in many countries of Asia.

Admission of converts to religious life without sufficient time to grow in Christian maturity also poses difficulties for the spirituality of Asian religious. Tendencies towards some sort of "fundamentalism" and return to pre-Vatican II ways may be detected among some religious under the influence of foreign institutes that have been scouring the "Asian markets" for religious vocations. On the other hand, religious more exposed to the modern or post-modern cultures, are running the risk of being overcome by the individualistic ethic, the work-orientation, the stress on efficiency, the drive to produce and the "spiritual supermarket" mentality that characterize the global market economy. These are likewise affecting the spiritual life of Asian religious and posing challenges to their efforts to be *mystics.*

In the face of these challenges, taking up the challenge of inculturating the faith/charism offers hope. Inculturation of the charism was one of the major strands in the discussions at the 1994 Synod on Consecrated Life and the 1998 Synod on Asia. A workshop was devoted to it at the 2004 Congress on Consecrated Life and John Paul II dealt with it in *Vita Consecrata* and *Ecclesia in Asia*. But in many ways, efforts towards inculturation of the faith/charism among religious in Asia "remain timid."

Prophets. A challenge for religious that rings loud and clear in Asia is the challenge for them to be credible *prophets* and counter-cultural witnesses. After forty years of Vatican II renewal, religious in Asia are in a better position to assess their prophetic impact. They have begun to realize that consecrated persons in Asia have created for themselves an image of very competent and dedicated professionals but not so much that of poor, simple, spiritual leaders. In their attempt to adapt to the modern world and to recover the incarnational dimension of religious life—neglected for so long before Vatican II—they have unconsciously compromised the counter cultural character of religious life by indiscriminately accepting what modernity and post modernity have to offer. On the other hand, some have absolutized an ideal Asian culture of the past to which they continue to hold on to, ignoring all demands for change. Both situations call Asian religious to a prophetic response.

The efforts of many religious soon after Vatican II to return to their biblical and charismatic sources according to the exhortations of *Perfectae Caritatis* (PC 2) have resulted in the rediscovery of the prophetic element as an essential dimension in the life of Jesus and of founders/foundresses. Some institutes—particularly international institutes—undertook serious, systematic efforts towards refounding as a result of this movement "to return to the sources." A renewal deeply anchored in the spirit of the founders/foundresses is essential if religious institutes are to confront the challenges of contemporary societies.

In many places in Asia, an "alternative modern culture" is gradually eroding the innate religiosity characteristic of Asian peoples. Elements in Asian cultures that have so far supported well the development of the spiritual life of Asians (e.g. the family, churches, religious institutions, the community) are being weakened by excessive and uncritical exposure to the influence of the modern and post-modern cultures of the West. The idol of technology has well installed itself in the altars of many religious communities without much difficulty. Frequently, the mission has been used to provide a convenient and facile excuse for it and the availability of resources has greatly facilitated it. The resulting secularism and materialism pose serious threats to religious in Asia.

Vis-à-vis these realities, Asian religious are being challenged to show more clearly the primacy of God and of the spiritual in their lives, to live their vows joyfully—individually and as communities—so as to offer "new cultural models" (cf. VC 80) that can fulfill the longing for fuller life of Asian peoples. In the Asian context, a poverty that visibly shows where the "treasure" of religious lies and an asceticism that enables them "to suffer with" their brothers and sisters without falling into hopelessness or passive resignation in the face of the crushing poverty of millions and the powerlessness this engenders, is a very powerful prophetic witness. Such prophetic witness is impossible without a deep Paschal spirituality that enables one to embrace the cross borne by "crucified Asian peoples" while having one's eyes fixed on the resurrection.

The modern culture that is sweeping across many parts of Asia has reduced people's "model of a good life" to the five Cs (car, cash, cell phone, credit card and condominium). A sense of the provisional characterizes the postmodern generation. In the face of this reality, the religious' life-long commitment to give themselves unreservedly to God and to the service of their brothers and sisters offers a powerful witness and an alternative model of what a "good life" means. Religious can demonstrate by their lives what "wholeness" and true "self-fulfillment" are and how they can be attained.

The primacy of God in the lives of consecrated persons and their single-minded following of Christ brings a unity to their lives that is a powerful prophetic statement in the face of the fragmentation of today's cultures. Furthermore, for Asians this transparency and simplicity of life in religious leaders is a sign of holiness. In the face of a modern Asia that values people for "what they do," as work forces, as economic units in the world market, religious can offer a counter witness. By the way they live, they can be a prophetic witness to the primacy of being (*who we are*) over doing (*what we do*); they can eloquently proclaim that even those who can no longer contribute through their work—the sick, the poor, the elderly—continue to be important and to merit our care.

In many Asian countries, women count among the most oppressed and exploited. The prophetic witness of women religious, totally given to God and to others without distinction of culture, religion or gender and who are taking their responsibilities in the Church and in their institutes seriously, is an irreplaceable witness in Asia. Their fellow Asian women need to see that their dream for a "new order" that fulfills their longing for participation, freedom and a more dignified life, is possible.

The exercise of authority and leadership in the spirit of Jesus who came "to serve and not to be served" is another much needed witness by consecrated persons. The triple dialogue enjoined by the Church in Asia will be facilitated if consecrated persons exercise their authority in a spirit of humble and loving service. Such an exercise of authority is a powerful prophetic witness in a continent where people have continually witnessed authoritarianism, abuse of power and domination.

If the witnessing of religious in Asia were to be prophetic, I personally believe that it needs to be radical, visible, effective and credible; "*Radical* because it reaches to the roots of our being: our desires, our affections, our values, our attitudes and our relationships. *Visible* because those around us can see it. Visibility in our context today implies the witness of communities and institutions, not only of individuals. *Effective* because it presents alternatives to ways of living that do not promote fullness of life. *Credibility* calls for consistency, integrity and harmony between words and deeds, proclamation and life" (see *FABC Papers 116,* pp. 42-43). Asian peoples must be able to "read" the witnessing of religious. This "readability" will depend on whether religious share the language, symbols, meanings, the hopes, struggles and dreams of their people for a better life.

Prophetic communities that live in solidarity with those that suffer, that create physical and spiritual spaces for dialogue and that are rooted in the charism of their founders are signs of hope in Asia today. Organized congregational efforts towards a spiritual renewal that grounds consecrated life in a solid spirituality and a deeper understanding of the world today, as well as formation programs that prepare religious for their prophetic vocation and the example of prophetic leaders, are still other signs of hope.

In a continent that has not been spared the pain of division— whether social, political or religious—the witness of multicultural and international communities living in mutual respect, acceptance and where differences are viewed as enrichment rather than problems, is a powerful prophetic symbol. And so is the silent and humble witness of consecrated persons who continue to be faithful in the midst of persecutions and dangers to their lives in some Asian countries. The example of countless Asian martyrs who shed their blood for the faith is a tremendous source of inspiration for Asian religious when the demands of prophecy begin to cost.

Prophecy calls for radicality, depth, courage and daring to be different. Obstacles to genuine prophecy can come from our Asian cultures. The tendency in the modern culture towards superficiality and the fear of confrontation, the tendency towards conformity in some traditional Asian cultures pose difficulties for would-be Asian prophets. The comfortable lifestyle of many religious and the complacency this engenders are other obstacles to be overcome.

Responding to the challenge of putting on the face of a *servant-mystic-prophet* will not be possible for consecrated persons in Asia unless they return to the "sources of the whole of the Christian life and to the primitive inspiration of the institutes" (PC 2), to recover the essentials of consecrated life and to reinterpret or to re-express them in today's cultural context. "Creative fidelity" imposes this on them.

Today this return to the sources needs to go beyond the efforts that were taken soon after Vatican II to adapt various aspects of consecrated life to the conditions of today's world (cf. PC 8, 10, 20). Beyond adaptation, religious are asked to inculturate consecrated life (cf. VC 80; EA 22). Inculturation entails returning to the fundamental meanings and values of consecrated life and re-expressing them in forms that are in harmony with the religious' cultural contexts. It implies assuming cultural elements compatible with consecrated life so that cultures and consecrated life can mutually enrich each other.

The charge of having a "foreign face" rests heavy on Christians and consecrated persons in many parts of Asia. Some international institutes are still clearly marked by their cultures of origin (e.g. in their lifestyle, formation, use of language, methods of evangelization, forms of ministry, ways of praying and administrative structures/practices). With inculturation, religious will give a distinctive Asian profile to their face as *servant-mystic-prophet*. It will transform them from *being religious in Asia* to *being Asian religious*. It will lead them to greater dynamism and renewal of life, works, spirituality, structures and governance, and the transformation of cultures. In a word, a "notable enrichment and a new season of spiritual and apostolic growth" (SAC 19) will be its fruit.

There are efforts on the part of religious in Asia to reflect on the inculturation of consecrated life and to realize it in the concrete, for example in lifestyle, formation, and other areas. But so much more needs to be done. Inculturating consecrated life in Asia cannot be separated from the challenges of solidarity, communion, dialogue, spirituality and prophecy. Responding to these challenges will help ensure an inculturated consecrated life.

Attempts at inculturation are not without difficulties. First among these is the mistaken notion that inculturation is a task for specialists. But, if inculturation involves an exchange or a dialogue between culture and consecrated life so that the culture feels at home with consecrated life and consecrated life finds a home in the culture, then inculturation can only happen at the level of daily life. The reflection by experts that is a necessary part of the process is not at the beginning of the inculturation process. Secondly, inculturating consecrated life calls for discernment. Inculturation is a challenge, whatever the stage of development of the culture, but it becomes even more difficult in the face of the multiculturalism and the cultural fragmentation that characterize many societies today. Inculturation does not absolutize cultures or make them the norm for one's choices and decisions. For this not to happen, there is need for discernment. A weak formation in discernment will make authentic inculturation very difficult, if not impossible.

To respond to the many challenges posed to consecrated life in Asia today, there is a great need for formators and leaders that are attuned to these challenges, creative in their reflection and courageous in their action. Formation must focus on developing values essential for consecrated life and on motivating religious to make choices that are value-based. An unfortunate tendency among some institutes faced by the numerous challenges confronting them today is for them to be satisfied with formation programs rich in "content" but weak or inadequate with regard to formation in evangelical and charism "values."

An inculturated and contextualized formation remains a major concern for Asian consecrated persons. For those in countries that have been cut off from the renewal initiated by Vatican II due to changes in political regimes, formation has tried to make up for "lost time" even as the challenges of continually and rapidly changing Asian societies do not leave much time. The same may be said of institutes in "young Churches" or of those that have converts among their members. The reality of a weak faith foundation due to an inadequate formation coupled at the same time by complex challenges from their rapidly evolving societies, poses sobering questions for the future of some institutes, notwithstanding a dramatic rise in the number of their members.

Today, more than ever, leaders of religious institutes in Asia are called to creative leadership that is equipped with a keen sense of discernment as to where the Spirit is blowing in society and in the Churches of Asia. They must ensure that the values that can transform religious into true *servants-mystics-prophets* are the focus of formation in their institutes and that the needed structures to promote them are in place. Becoming a *servant-mystic-prophet* is a life-long process that can either be aided tremendously by appropriate formation processes and community structures or hindered by the absence of the same.

Towards the Future ... with Hope. The path of renewal for consecrated life mapped out by Vatican II over forty years ago has proven irreversible. Subsequent developments in the Asian continent have shown this. As consecrated persons in Asia contemplate their future in a continent and in a world that have been undergoing a dramatic "change of era," they are conscious that they are living in a special "time of grace both for the Church and for consecrated life" in the continent today.

John Paul II in his Apostolic Exhortation after the Asian Synod wrote: "The search for God, a life of fraternal communion, and service to others are the three chief characteristics of the consecrated life which can offer an appealing Christian testimony to the peoples of Asia today. The Special Assembly for Asia urged those in consecrated life to be witnesses to the universal call to holiness and inspiring examples to Christians and non-Christians alike of self-giving love for everyone, especially the least of their brothers and sisters" (EA 44). Asian women and men religious that wear the face of a *servant-mystic-prophet* embody well these characteristics and respond to this call. They will be capable of fascinating and drawing to Him whom they love, millions of Asian peoples who are searching for Him in ways that are unknown even to themselves. This will be their irreplaceable contribution in shaping the "new Asia" that is being born today and in realizing the hope that in the third millennium *"a great harvest of faith* will be reaped in this vast and vital continent" (EA 1). [NOTE: This text was received in late 2005; sincere gratitude is expressed to the author for her contribution. – Editor]

COMMON ABBREVIATIONS

EA – *Ecclesia in Asia*
FAPA I – *For All the Peoples of Asia,* Volume I (1992)
FAPA II – *For All the Peoples of Asia,* Volume II (1997)
FAPA III – *For All the Peoples of Asia,* Volume III (2002)
IL:SA – *Instrumentum Laboris:* Synod for Asia
LG – *Lumen Gentium*
M:SA – Message: Synod for Asia
NMI – *Novo Millennio Ineunte*
PC – *Perfectae Caritatis*
SAC – *Starting Afresh from Christ*
VC – *Vita Consecrata*

12

RECEPTION OF VATICAN II IN ASIA
Historical and Theological Analysis

Peter C. Phan

The Second Vatican Ecumenical Council has been characterized as the most significant event of the twentieth century, both in secular and ecclesiastical history. Given the extensive reforms it has spawned in the Roman Catholic Church worldwide and its ramifications for ecumenical unity and the society at large, the description seems by no means overblown.

While Vatican II's impact on the Western Churches is clearly discernible and has been subjected to frequent evaluations,[1] whether and to what extent the Council has influenced the Churches in other parts of the world has not been extensively documented. The purpose of this chapter is to determine and

---

[1]The literature, especially theological, is immense. On the official level, Pope John Paul II convoked an Extraordinary Synod of Bishops on the 20th anniversary of the closing of the Council (24 November to 8 December 1985) to take stock of the conciliar reforms. Though not official, Josef Ratzinger's assessment of Vatican II in his *The Ratzinger Report* (San Francisco: Ignatius Press, 1985), an interview with Vittorio Messori, is influential, given his position as Prefect of the Congregation of the Doctrine of the Faith [and now as Pope Benedict XVI]. Among theological evaluations is the massive three-volume

evaluate Vatican II's impact on the Churches of Asia.[2] Such an evaluation is extremely complex, not only because the field of enquiry is so vast, and theological bibliography scarce, but also because in many countries empirical data on the Churches' activities are practically impossible to obtain.[3] Furthermore, the expression "Vatican II" is itself highly ambiguous, and of course, unless there is a consensus on what is meant by "Vatican II," an evaluation of its impact on the Churches of Asia would lack a clear focus.[4]

---

work edited by René Latourelle, *Vatican II: Assessment and Perspectives. Twenty-five Years After (1962-1987)*, published simultaneously in several European languages. The English edition was brought out by Paulist Press, 1988. A helpful assessment of Vatican II is Giuseppe Alberigo, Jean-Pierre Jossua and Joseph Komonchak (eds.), *The Reception of Vatican II*, also published in several languages. The English translation is by Matthew J. O'Connell, published by The Catholic University Press of America, 1987, hereafter cited as *Reception*. Other helpful general works include: Alberic Stacpoole (ed.), *Vatican II Revisited By Those Who Were There*, (Minneapolis, MN: Winston Press, 1986); F. X. Kaufmann and A. Zingerle (eds.), *Vatikanum II und Modernisierung: Historische, Theolologische und Soziologische Perspektiven* (Paderborn: Schöning, 1996); and David Tracy, with Hans Küng and Johann B. Metz (eds.), *Toward Vatican III: The Work That Needs To Be Done* (New York: The Seabury Press, 1978).

[2]By Asian Churches here is meant primarily the Roman Catholic Churches of the Indian subcontinent and of the Far East (excluding the Churches of the Near and Middle East and of Central Asia). These Churches (and others) form part of the Federation of Asian Bishops' Conferences (FABC), about which more will be said below.

[3]This is particularly true of Churches under the communist regime, such as mainland China, North Korea, and Vietnam.

[4]It will be suggested below that "Vatican II" should be taken in a comprehensive sense.

With these limitations in mind, I will begin with a brief overview of Vatican II and the current situation of Asian Catholic Churches. I will next examine the various areas of Church life in Asia in which the Council has exercised a significant influence, with reference to the achievements of the organization named the Federation of Asian Bishops' Conferences (FABC). I will end by offering a theological evaluation of the Council's impact by examining one of the most important events in the life of the Asian Churches, namely, the Special Assembly of the Synod of Bishops for Asia.[5]

Vatican II and the Asian Churches. Announced by Pope John XXIII to the consternation and thinly veiled opposition of his advisers on 25 January 1959 and formally convoked on 25 December 1961, the Second Vatican Council opened on 11 October 1962. Suspended by Pope John's death on 3 June 1963 and continued by Pope Paul VI, the Council concluded on 8 December 1965. The Council issued 16 documents of various levels of authority (4 constitutions, 9 decrees, and 3 declarations).[6] Of these documents, it is generally agreed that dogmatically speaking, the most important is the dogmatic constitution on the Church (*Lumen Gentium*); in terms of immediate impact on Church life, the constitution on the liturgy (*Sacrosanctum Concilium*) is the most significant; and in terms of the influence on the society at large, the pastoral constitution on the Church on the modern world (*Gaudium et Spes*) is the most influential. In addition, for Asia, given its multireligious

---

[5]This presentation is by design predominantly *bibliographical.* It is intended to be a modest contribution to the history of the post-Vatican II Catholic Church in Asia, which remains largely unwritten.

[6]For an English translation, see ed. Austin Flannery, ed., *Vatican Council II*, New Revised Edition (Collegeville, MN: Liturgical Press, 1975). English translation of Vatican II's documents in this chapter is taken from this work.

context and the Church's minority status, the decree on the Church's missionary activity (*Ad Gentes*) and the declaration on the relationship of the Church to non-Christian religions (*Nostra Aetate*) are of particular relevance.

To form a correct assessment of Vatican II, it is important to recall that Vatican II was intended by Pope John XXIII to be a "pastoral" council.[7] Instead of being "a discussion of one article or another of the fundamental doctrine of the Church," the Council was directed to make "a step forward toward a doctrinal penetration and a formation of consciousness in faithful and perfect conformity to the authentic doctrine...."[8] The question to ask when assessing Vatican II's impact on the Asian Churches is therefore not whether in the post-conciliar period they have produced new doctrines but whether they have achieved a deeper understanding of the Christian faith and formed a keener consciousness of their Christian identity and mission in conformity with their faith.[9]

Another factor to be kept in mind is that Vatican II itself could not of course implement its own reform programs and

[7]Giuseppe Alberigo has usefully warned against a misunderstanding of the "pastoral" character of Vatican II, taking it to mean excluding or minimizing the importance of doctrines. See *Reception*, 16, footnote 53. Alberigo explains: "By using this adjective, then, he [John XXIII] was giving Vatican II an ecclesial scope that was not solely dogmatic or solely disciplinary but all-embracing" (17).

[8]Pope John XXIII's Opening Speech to the Council. English text in Walter Abbott, ed., *The Documents of Vatican II* (New York: Guild Press, 1966), 715.

[9]On this point see the many works of John F. Kobler, in particular his *Vatican II, Theophany and the Phenomenon of Man: The Council's Pastoral Servant Leader Theology for the Third Millennium* (New York: Peter Lang, 1991).

therefore called for the establishment of various post-conciliar commissions (e.g., the Consilium for the Implementation of the Constitution on the Liturgy) and secretariats (e.g., Secretariats for the Promotion of Christian Unity, for Non-Christian Religions, and for Non-Believers) to devise concrete ways and measures to carry out the Church reform instituted by the Council. It is reasonable then that in assessing the impact of "Vatican II" attention should not be limited to the event of the conciliar meeting itself nor to its 16 documents but must link them to the official post-conciliar documents (e.g., numerous liturgical books, the new Code of Canon Law, the *Catechism of the Catholic Church*, etc.), and institutions, indeed, to the entire pontificates of Paul VI and John Paul II.

Vatican II was the first ecumenical Council that the Asian bishops took part in, though many of them were not Asian-born but expatriate missionaries. Nor did their voices carry much weight, since Vatican II—though the first general Council truly represented by the *oikoumene* and hence ushering in the "world church"[10]—was still very much an European affair, dominated by European prelates and the preoccupations of the Western Churches. This lack of influence was due to the fact that the number of Asian bishops was relatively small and that many Asian Churches were still in mission lands. This minority status of Christianity in Asia, except in the Philippines, with all its disadvantages, must be taken into account when we will note that Vatican II had not achieved its impact on the Asian Churches as it could have.

It would be useful then, before we embark upon a study of the reception of Vatican II by the Asian Churches, to take a brief

---

[10]This is Karl Rahner's famous interpretation of Vatican II. See his "Towards a Fundamental Theological Interpretation of Vatican II," *Theological Studies* 40 (1979), 716-27.

look at their current situation. In Asia, Catholics (105.2 million in 1997) represent only 2.9% of the nearly 3.5 billion Asians. Moreover, well over 50% of all Asian Catholics are found in one country—the Philippines. Thus, if one excludes the Philippines, Asia is only about one percent Catholic. Despite its extreme minority status, the Catholic Church in Asia continues to grow. In 1988 there were 84.3 million Catholics. By 1997 they had reached 105.2 million (an increase of 20.9 million or 25%). It is also interesting to note that most of the Asian clergy and religious are indigenous: in 1997 Asia had 617 bishops (out of 4,420 bishops in the world) and 32,291 priests (17,789 diocesan and 14,502 religious). Two-third of all religious priests are Asian; the vast majority of religious sisters (88%) are also Asian.[11] Needless to say, this numerical minority as well as other political, economic and religious factors have impeded a full implementation of Vatican II in Asia. On the other hand, these situations have also shaped the particular ways in which the Asian Churches responded to Vatican II's call for reform.

---

[11]For resources on statistics of the Asian Churches, consult *Catholic Almanac* (Our Sunday Visitor, Inc.), *Statistical Yearbook of the Church* (Vatican Press), and "Annual Statistical Table on Global Mission," in the first number of each volume of *International Bulletin of Missionary Research.* For statistics of Catholics in individual countries belonging to the Federation of Asian Bishops' Conferences, the following data are given, with the name of the country, its estimated population in millions for the year 2000, and the percentage of Catholics: *Bangladesh* (145.8/0.27%); *Bhutan* (1.8/0.02%); *Burma/ Myanmar* (48.8/1.3%); *Cambodia* (10.3/0.02%); *China* (1,239.5/0.5%); *Hong Kong* (6.9/4.7%); *India* (990/1.72%); *Indonesia* (202/2.58%); *Japan* (127.7/0.36%); *North Korea* (22.6/?); *South Korea* (47.2/6.7%); *Laos* (6.2/0.9%); *Macau* (0.5/5%); *Malaysia* (22/3%); *Mongolia* (2.5/?); *Nepal* (23/0.05%); *Pakistan* (142.6/0.8%); *Philippines* (74.8/81%); *Singapore* (3.1/6.5%); *Sri Lanka* (20.8/8%); *Taiwan* (22.1/1.4%); *Thailand* (61.6/0.4%); *Vietnam* (78.2/6.1). I am grateful to James H. Kroeger, MM, for these statistics.

The Reception of Vatican II in Asia. 1. The first way in which the Asian Churches received the Second Vatican Council was to translate its 16 Latin documents into their own languages. While this task was somewhat easy for countries where English is by and large the second language (e.g., the Philippines and India), it posed considerable challenges to Churches in countries where even a basic Christian vocabulary was not yet available, let alone highly technical theological and canonical terms, and where experts in both theology and the local languages were in short supply. In these cases most often the translation of the conciliar documents was equivalent to an appropriation and inculturation of the theological orientations of the Council itself. Hence, the translations were themselves major theological achievements of the Asian Churches.[12]

2. It is universally agreed that the most immediate and visible impact of Vatican II was its liturgical reforms, not only with its encouragement of the use of vernaculars in liturgical celebrations but also thanks to a slew of post-conciliar new liturgical books (e.g., missal, liturgy of the hours, rituals, and pontifical) composed by the Consilium for the implementation of

---

[12]The following translations, beside English, are available: Chinese: *Chiao hui hsien chang: fu shih* (T'ai-chung: Kuang ch'i ch'u pan che, 1966) [Taiwanese] (early translation); *Fan-ti-kang ti erh chieh ta kung hui I wen hsien* (T'ai pei: Chung-kuo chu chiao t'uan mi shu ch'u ch'u pan: T'ien chu chiao chiao wu hsieh chin ch'u pan she, 1979) [revised translation]. Korean: *Che -ch'a Pat'ik'an Konguihoe munhon: honjang, kyoryong, sononmun* (Seoul T'ukpyolsi: Han'guk Ch'onjugyo Chungang Hyobuihoe, 1969). Bahasa Indonesia: *Dokumen Konsili Vatikan II* (Jakarta: Dokpen KWI dan Obor, 1993). Vietnamese: *Thanh Cong Dong Chung Vaticano II*, in two volumes: Volume 1: *Hien che, Sac lenh, Tuyen ngon, Su diep.* Volume 2: *Ban muc luc. Phan tich chu de. Trung dan tai lieu* (Da Lat: Phan Khoa Than Hoc Giao Hoang Hoc Vien Thanh Pio X, 1972). There are also Bengali, Japanese, and Thai translations.

the Constitution on the Liturgy established by Pope Paul VI in 1964. The goal of the reforms is to promote a "full, conscious, and active participation in liturgical celebrations" (SC 14). Once again, the task of translating these liturgical books was a daunting one, but there is no doubt that with the use of vernaculars and the new rites, the faithful in Asia were enabled to achieve a full, conscious and active participation in the liturgical celebrations that had not been possible before the Council.

3. The reception of Vatican II's liturgical reforms in Asia, however, went far beyond the translation of the liturgical books composed by the Roman authorities into vernaculars. It included also an explicit effort of liturgical inculturation by bringing elements of the local cultures into sacramental and liturgical celebrations. This inculturation occurs at many levels. On a more superficial level, it includes the use of local music and songs, vestments, gestures, rituals, sacred objects, architecture.[13] On a deeper level, it involves the composition

---

[13]In India, the person most responsible for the process of liturgical reform was no doubt Duraisamy Simon Amalorpavadass. Only a representative bibliography on liturgical adaptation in Asia since Vatican II can be given here. See Michael Amaladoss, "Musique et rite en Inde," *La Maison-Dieu* 108 (1971), 138-42; "Adaptation in Liturgy and the Problem of Meaning," in *God's Word among Men*, ed. G. Gispert-Sauch (Dehli: Vidyajyoti, 1973), 305-14; idem, "Liturgy and Creativity: Fourth All-India Liturgical Meeting," *Clergy Monthly* (henceforth, *CM*) 38 (1974), 124-33; idem, "Liturgical Adaptation in the Light of History," *Word and Worship* (henceforth, *WW*) 8 (1975), 381-91; idem, "Liturgical Renewal and Ecclesiastical Law," *WW* 10 (1977), 249-60; idem, "The Liturgy: Twenty Years After Vatican II," *Vidyayjoti Journal of Theological Reflection* (henceforth, *VJTR*) 47 (1983), 231-39; idem, "Relaunching the Indian Liturgy: Some Reflections on Our Experiment," *VJTR* 49 (1985), 446-55; idem, "Ritualità, teologia, cultura. Una reflessione sull'inculturazione nella liturgia," *La Civiltà Cattolica* 4276 (1986), 440-54; Duraisamy Simon Amalorpavadass, "Liturgy and Catechetics in

of new sacramental rituals for significant events in a person's life such as marriage and funerals.[14] It sometimes includes the

---

India Today," *Teaching All Nations* (henceforth, *TAN*) 6/4 (1969), 378-88; idem, *Towards Indigenization in the Liturgy* (Bangalore: National Biblical, Catechetical & Liturgical Centre/St. Paul Press, 1971); idem (ed.), *Post-Vatican Liturgical Renewal in India at All Levels, Vol. 2: 1968-1971* (Bangalore: National Biblical, Catechetical and Liturgical Centre, 1972); idem (ed.), *Post-Vatican Liturgical Renewal in India at All Levels During a Decade, Vol. 3: 1963-1973* (Bangalore: National Biblical, Catechetical & Liturgical Centre, 1976); idem (ed.), *Post-Vatican Liturgical Renewal in India at All Levels, Vol. 4: 1974-1976* (Bangalore: National Biblical, Catechetical & Liturgical Centre, 1977); Jos De Cuyper, "First All-India Liturgical Meeting," *CM* 32 (1968), 221-24; idem, "The Future of the Liturgy in India," *CM* 33 (1969), 525-37; Jacques Dupuis, "Second All-India Liturgical Meeting," *CM* 33 (1969), 219-23; idem, "Christ and the Holy Spirit in Liturgical Worship," *CM* 35 (1971), 190-98; idem, "Planning the Liturgy of Tomorrow (Third All-India Liturgical Meeting)," *CM* 36 (1972), 93-105; Tissa Balasuriya, "Renewal of the Liturgy in Asia," *CM* 32 (1968), 53-64 [Part I], 121-29 [Part II]; idem, "Renewal of the Liturgy in Asia," *TAN* 5/2 (1968), 175-99; idem, *The Eucharist and Human Liberation* (Maryknoll, NY: Orbis Books, 1979); Eduardo P. Hontiveros, "Composing Music for an Asian Local Church," *EAPR* 19 (1982), 38-47; Anscar J. Chupungco, *Liturgical Renewal in the Philippines: Maryhill Liturgical Consultations* (Quezon City, Philippines: Maryhill School of Theology, 1980); idem, *Towards a Filipino Liturgy* (Quezon City, Philippines: Maryhill School of Theology, 1976); idem, "A Filipino Attempt at Liturgical Inculturation," *Ephemerides Liturgicae* 91 (1977), 370-76; idem, "A Filipino Adaptation of the Liturgical Language," in *Eulogia Miscellanea Liturgica in Onore di P. Burkhard Neunheuser, O.S.B.* (Roma: Editrice Anselmiana, 1979), 45-55; idem, *Liturgical Renewal in the Philippines* (Quezon City, Philippines: Maryhill Theological School, 1980); idem, "Liturgical Inculturation," *EAPR* 30 (1993), 108-19; Subhash Anand, "The Inculturation of the Eucharistic Liturgy," *VJTR* 57 (1993), 269-93.

[14]See Anton Pain Ratu, "A Proposed Marriage Rite for Dawanese Catholics," [Part 1], *TAN*, 11 (1974), 3-21; [Part II], 99-119; Peter

use of sacred writings in addition to the Christian Scriptures.[15] In some countries, sacred rituals such as the cult of ancestors are incorporated into the liturgy.[16] Because of their academic resources and favorable political conditions, two countries have

---

Knecht, "Funerary Rites and the Concept of Ancestors in Japan: A Challenge to the Christian Churches?" in R. Hardawiryana, et al., *Building the Church in Pluricultural Asia.* Inculturation: Working Papers on Living Faith and Cultures, Vol. 7 (Rome: Centre "Cultures and Religions"—Pontifical Gregorian University, 1986), 121-44; T. Pereira, *Towards an Indian Christian Indian Funeral Rite* (Bangalore: National Biblical, Catechetical & Liturgical Centre, 1980); R. Serrano, "Toward a Cultural Adaptation of the Rite of Marriage," S.T.D. dissertation, Pontifical Liturgical Institute of San Anselmo, Rome, 1987; Thomas Cherukat, "Christian Sacraments and Hindu Samskaras: A Theological of Baptism and Confirmation Compared to the Hindu Initiation Rite of Upanayana Samskara in the Context of Inculturation and Interreligious Dialogue in India." Ph.D. dissertation, University of Vienna, Austria, 1991.

[15]See Michael Amaladoss, "Textes hindous dans la prière chrétienne," *Christus* 67 (1970), 424-32; idem, "Text and Context: The Place of Non-Biblical Readings in the Liturgy," in Duraisamy Simon Amalorpavadass (ed.), *Research Seminar on Non-Biblical Scriptures* (Bangalore: National Biblical, Catechetical and Liturgical Centre, 1974), 210-21; idem, "Non-Biblical Scriptures in Christian Life and Worship," *JJTR* 39 (1975), 194-209; G. Gispert-Sauch, "Sacred Scriptures in Indian Religions," *VJTR* 39 (1975), 217-22; Virginia K. Kennerley, "The Use of Indigenous Sacred Literature and Theological Concept in Christian Eucharistic Liturgy in India," *Studia Liturgica* 19 (1989), 143-61.

[16]See the documents of the Vietnamese bishops on the veneration of ancestors and heroes on 14 June 1965 and on 14 November 1974. The Vietnamese text of the former declaration is printed in *Sacerdos* (Saigon) 43 (1965), 489-92 and its French translation is found in *Documentation Catholique* 63 (1966), col. 467-70.

made significant contributions to the reception of Vatican II's liturgical reform in general, that is, India and the Philippines.[17]

4. Liturgical inculturation is only an aspect of the larger enterprise which Vatican II has spawned in Asia, perhaps more extensively than anywhere else in the Catholic world. Whereas the Catholic Church in Latin America has been more concerned with the socio-economic oppression of the poor and marginalized, and hence was more focused on *liberation*, Asian Christians, while also concerned with the issues of justice, as we shall see below, have been more engaged the *inculturation* of the Christian faith. Of course, these two aspects—liberation and inculturation—are not understood as two competing and unrelated tasks. Indeed, it is a fundamental axiom of Asian theologians and the FABC that they cannot and must not be separated from each other. Liberation without inculturation suffers from a truncated anthropology which sees humans simply as economic beings, while inculturation without liberation

---

[17]For an assessment of India: See Louis Maliekal, "Liturgical Inculturation in India: Problems and Prospects of Experimentation,"*Jeevadhara* 18 (1988), 279-92; Antony Nariculam, "The Liturgical Crisis in the Syro-Malabar Church," *Jeevadhara* 18 (1988), 293-302; J. Saldanha, "Liturgical Adaptation in India: 1963-1974," *VJTR* 40 (1976), 20-31; Paul Puthanangady, "Inculturation of the Liturgy in India since Vatican II," in Mary Collins and David Power, eds., *Liturgy: A Creative Tradition.* Concilium, vol. 162 (New York: Seabury Press, 1983), 71-77; idem, "Liturgical Inculturation in India," *Jeevadhara* 23 (1993), 193-207; Jose Matthew Kakkallil, "Liturgical Inculturation in India," *Questions Liturgiques* 77 (1996), 109-116. For an assessment of the Philippines, see, besides the works of Chupungco, Paul William Diener, "The Philippines and Vatican II: The Impact of an Ecumenical Council," Ph.D. dissertation. Temple University, 1972; Julio X. Labayen, "Vatican II in Asia and the Philippines," *Ecumenical Review* 37/3 (1985), 275-82.

becomes an elitist, antiquarian quest irrelevant to people's lives.[18]

In terms of the reception of Vatican II, it may be said that while Latin American liberation theology privileges numbers 63-76 of the Pastoral Constitution on the Church in the Modern World,[19] the Asian Churches, living as they do in the midst of ancient, rich, and diverse cultures, focus on numbers 54-62.[20] From the existing literature, there is no doubt that inculturation has occupied the lion's share of Asian theologians. This is true particularly of India[21] and the

---

[18]This thesis has been powerfully asserted by Aloysius Pieris. See his *An Asian Theology of Liberation* (Maryknoll, NY: Orbis Books, 1988).

[19]*Gaudium et Spes*, nos. 63-72 speak of economic and social life, and nos. 73-76 of the political community.

[20]*Gaudium et Spes*, nos. 54-62 speak of cultural situations today and some more urgent duties of Christians in regard to culture.

[21]The bibliography is immense. For India, see G. Gispert-Sauch, "Towards an Indian Theology," *CM* 33 (1969), 547-51; idem, "Towards an Indian Theology," *CM* 35 (1971), 262-64; Samuel Ryan, "An Indian Christology: A Discussion of Method," *Jeevadhara* 1/3 (1971), 212-27; idem, "Inculturation and People's Struggles," *Indian Missiological Review* (henceforth, *IMR*) 19/1 (1997), 33-45; Michael Amaladoss, "Inculturation: Theological Perspectives," *Jeevadhara* 6 (1976), 293-302; idem, "Theologizing in India Today," *VJTR* 43 (1979), 213-25; idem, "Inculturation and the Tasks of Mission," *EAPR* 17/2 (1980), 117-25; idem, "Inculturation in India," *EAPR* 18 (1981), 320-30; idem, "L'Église en Inde: Vingt ans après Vatican II," in Paul Ladrière & René Luneau, eds., *Le Retour des certitudes* (Paris: Centurion, 1987), 13-33; idem, *Becoming Indian: The Process of Inculturation* (Rome: Center for Indian and International Studies, 1992); idem, "Inculturation in India: Historical Perspectives and Questions," *Yearbook of Contextual Theologies 1994* (Aachen: Missio, 1994), 42-58; idem, "The Gospel,

Philippines.[22] However, Churches in other countries have
not neglected this aspect of Christian mission: Japan,[23]

Community and Culture: Inculturation in Tamil Nadu (India) Today,"
Zeitschrift für Missionswissenschaft und Religionswissenschaft 80
(1996), 179-89; idem, *Beyond Inculturation: Can the Many Be One?*
(Delhi, India: Indian Society for Promoting Christian Knowledge,
1998); Duraisamy Simon Amalorpavadas, "Theological Reflections
on Inculturation," *Studia Liturgica* 20/1 (1990), 36-54 [Part I], 116-36
[Part II]; Sebastian Elavathingal, *Inculturation and Christian Art: An
Indian Perspective* (Rome: Urbaniana University Press, 1990); Josef
Neuner, "Indisierung oder Hinduisierung der Kirche? Problem der
Inkulturation in Indien," *Die Katholischen Missionen* 106 (1987), 189-
95; Joseph Prasad Pinto, *Inculturation Through Basic Communities:
An Indian Perspective* (Bangalore: Asian Trading Corporation, 1985);
Arul M. Varaprasadam, "Inculturation: The Crucial Challenges in the
Indian Situation," in R. Hardawiryana, et al., *Building the Church in
Pluricultural Asia* (Rome: Centre "Cultures and Religions"—Pontifical
Gregorian University, 1986), 39-62; Subhash Anand, "Inculturation
in India: Yesterday, Today and Tomorrow," *IMR* 19/1 (1997), 19-
45; Kurien Kunnupuram, "Inculturation and Ecclesiology," *IMR* 19/1
(1997), 46-55; Kurien Kunnupuram & Lorenzo Fernando (eds.),
*Quest for an Indian Church: An Exploration of the Possibilities
Opened Up by Vatican II* (Anand, Gujarat, India: Gujarat Sahitya
Prakash, 1993); Gavin D'Costa, "Inculturation, India and Other
Religions: Some Methodological Reflections," *Studia Missionalia*
44 (1995), 121-47; Felix Wilfred, *From the Dusty Soil: Contextual
Reinterpretation of Christianity* (Madras: University of Madras, 1995);
idem, "Interkulturelle Begegnung statt Inkulturation: Prolegomena
zum Verstehen von Begegnungen zwischen Kultur und christlichem
Evangelium im Kontext Indiens/Asiens," *Jahrbuch Mission 1995*
(Hamburg: Missionshilfe Verlag, 1995), 114-33.

[22]See Leonardo Mercado, *Elements of Filipino Theology* (Tacloban
City: Divine Word University Publications, 1974); idem, *Inculturation
and Filipino Theology* (Manila: Divine Word Publication, 1992); idem,
Christ in the Philippines (Tacloban, Philippines: Divine Word University,
1982); Carlos Abesamis, "Doing Theological Reflection in a Philippine
Context," in Sergio Torres and Virginia Fabella (eds.), *The Emergent*

Indonesia,[24] Korea,[25] Malaysia,[26] Pakistan,[27] Sri Lanka,[28] Taiwan,[29] Thailand,[30] and Vietnam.[31] In light of these efforts

Gospel: Theology form the Underside of History (Maryknoll, NY: Orbis Books, 1978), 112-23; Ed Garcia, The Filipino Quest (Quezon City: Claretian Publications, 1988); A. B. Lambino, "Toward an Inculturated Theology in the Philippines," South East Asian Journal of Theology 20 (1979): 35-38; Ladislav Nemet, "Inculturation in the Philippines: A Theological Study of the Question of Inculturation in the Documents of CBCP and Selected Filipino Theologians in the Light of Vatican II and the Documents of the FABC." S.T.D. dissertation. Pontificia Universitas Gregoriana, 1994. Perhaps the most impressive fruit of the theological inculturation by the Filipino Church is the Catechism for Filipino Catholics (Manila: Word & Life Publications, 1997), produced by the Catholic Bishops' Conference of the Philippines. It has the distinction of being the first national catechism composed under the guidance of the Catechism of the Catholic Church and approved by Rome.

[23]See A. Takehiro Kunii, "Inculturation in Japan," EAPR 18 (1981), 337-42; Joseph Sasaski, "God's Word in Japanese Culture and Tradition," EAPR 17 (1980), 51-60; T.F. Tagaki, "Inculturation and Adaptation in Japan Before and After Vatican II," Catholic Historical Review 79/2 (1993), 246-67.

[24]See Hubertus J. W. M. Boelaars, "Indonesianisasi: Het omvormingsproces van de Katholieke Kerk in Indonesie tot de Indonesische Katholieke Kerk," Ph. D. Dissertation. Katholieke Universiteit Brabant (Netherlands), 1991; J.B. Banawiratma and Tom Jacobs, "Doing Theology with Local Resources: An Indonesian Experiment," EAPR 26 (1989), 51-72.

[25]See Luke Jong-Hyeok Sim, "A Theological Evaluation of Minjung Theology from the Perspective of Inculturation in Christianity," EAPR 29 (1992), 406-26; Philip You-Chul Kim, "Inculturation in the Process of Evangelization: With Reference to the Catholic Church in Korea." S.T.D. dissertation, Pontificia Universitas Lateranensis, 1996.

[26]See Jonathan Yun-ka Tan, "Toward a Theology of 'Muhibbah' as

at inculturation, it is clear that by implementing Vatican II's teaching, the Asian Churches have decisively moved away from the dominant model of mission as the *plantatio ecclesiae* of the pre-Vatican II era.

5. Another aspect of the Asian Churches, intimately intertwined with their efforts at liberation and inculturation, is their commitment to interreligious dialogue, and this, again, as a response to Vatican II. Among the Council's documents,

---

the Basis for Cross-Cultural Liturgical Inculturation in the Malaysian Catholic Church." MA Thesis. Graduate Theological Union, Berkeley, CA, 1997.

[27]See Anonymous, "Inculturation in the Light of Islam in Pakistan," *Pastoral Notes* 4 (1980), 114-24.

[28]See K. Lawrence, "Sri Lanka: Some Aspects of Inculturation," *EAPR* 18 (1981), 344-46; Aloysius Pieris, "Inculturation as a Missionary/Evangelical Presence in a Religiously Plural Society: Two Examples from Sri Lanka," *EAPR* 32 (1995), 81-86.

[29]See Antonio S. Samson (ed.), *Towards Indigenization of Religious Forms: Proceedings of the 1986 Workshop* (Manila: Association of Christian Universities and Colleges in Asia, 1986). This work contains essays on inculturation in Hong Kong, Indonesia, Japan, Korea, Philippines, Taiwan, and Thailand.

[30]See Saad Chaiwan, "A Study of Christian Mission in Thailand," *EAPR* 2/1 (1984), 62-74.

[31]See Peter C. Phan, "The Christ of Asia: An Essay on Jesus as the Eldest Son and Ancestor," *Studia Missionalia* 45 (1996), 25-55; idem, "Jesus as the Eldest Brother and Ancestor? A Vietnamese Portrait," *The Living Light* 33/1 (1996), 35-44; idem, "Doing Theology in the Context of Mission: Lessons from Alexandre de Rhodes," *Gregorianum* 81/4 (2000), 723-49.

the Declaration on the Relation of the Church to Non-Christian Religions (*Nostra Aetate*), though brief and of lesser ecclesiastical weight, has exercised a profound influence on the Asian Churches, since it is they (and not the Western Churches) that have to rub shoulders daily with followers of other religions, such as Buddhism, Confucianism, Islam, and Taoism, to mention only the religions that are found across Asia. Dialogue with other religions has become a constitutive dimension of the Church's evangelizing mission. This dialogue has assumed different forms: dialogue of life (common living as good neighbors), dialogue of action (collaboration for development and liberation), dialogue of theological exchange (understanding of different religious heritages), and dialogue of religious experience (sharing of spiritual riches).[32] These activities are being carried out on a daily basis by the Asian Churches throughout Asia, whenever social, political, and religious circumstances permit.[33]

---

[32]See *Dialogue and Proclamation: Reflections and Orientations on Interreligious Dialogue and the Proclamation of the Gospel of Jesus Christ* issued by the Pontifical Council for Interreligious Dialogue and the Congregation for the Evangelization of Peoples, nos. 42. The text is found in *Bulletin of the Pontifical Council for Interreligious Dialogue*, vol. 26, no. 2 (Rome: Vatican Polyglot Press, 1991).

[33]A representative bibliography is given here. Asandas D. Balchand, "The Salvific Value of Non-Christian Religions According to Asian Christian Theologians' Writings in Asian-Published Theological Journals, 1965-1970," *TAN* 10 (1973), 10-37 [Part I]; 115-52 [Part II]; Parmananda Divarkar, "Ecumenical Dialogue with Muslims," *Clergy Monthly Supplement* 8 (1967), 177-81; A. D'Souza, "Evangelization and Dialogue with Muslims," *CM* 38 (1974), 456-61; Mariasusai Dhavamony (ed.), *Evangelization, Dialogue and Development: Selected Papers of the International Theological Conference, Nagpur* (India), 1971 (Rome: Editrice Università Gregoriana, 1972); Josef Neuner, "The Place of World Religions in Theology," *CM* 32 (1968), 102-15; Michael

6. Another salient characteristic of the post-Vatican II Asian Churches is their engagement in the work of social development and liberation. Even before the Council they had been known for their work in education, health care and social services. However, in the past these activities, especially those in the field of education, were often carried out for the benefit of Catholics or as a means for proselytization. In the light of Vatican II, and under the influence of Latin American liberation theology, they are now seen as an integral part of the proclamation of the Good News, for and by the poor.[34] In recent times, Asian theologians

---

Amaladoss, *Faith, Culture and Inter-Religious Dialogue* (New Delhi: Indian Social Institute, 1985); idem, "The Pluralism of Religions and the Significance of Christ," *VJTR* 53 (1989), 401-20; idem, *Walking Together: The Practice of Inter-Religious Dialogue* (Anand, Gujarat, India: Gujarat Sahitya Prakash, 1992); idem, "The One and the Many: Reality and Manifestation," *Indian Theological Studies* 29 (1992), 305-28; idem, "Dialogue interreligieux et inculturarion du christianisme: Perspectives indiennes," *Revue de L'Institut Catholique de Paris* 51 (1994), 9-19; idem, "Inter-Religious Dialogue: A View from Asia," *Landas* 8 (1994), 208-18; Zacharias Paranilam, *Christian Openness to the World Religions: Catholic Approach to the World Religions according to* Nostra Aetate *of Vatican II with a Special Reference to Hinduism* (Kerala, India: Pontifical Institute Publications, 1988); J. Kuttianimattathil, *Practice and Theology of Interreligious Dialogue: A Critical Study of the Indian Christian Attempts Since Vatican II* (Bangalore, India: Kristu Jyoti College, 1995); Sebastian Painadath, "Theological Perspectives of FABC on Interreligious Dialogue," *Jeevadhara* 27 (1997), 272-88; George M. Soares-Prabhu, "The Indian Church Challenged by Pluralism and Dialogue," *SEDOS Bulletin* 26 (1994), 171-82; Felix Wilfred, "Some Tentative Reflections on the Language of Christian Uniqueness: An Indian Perspective," *Bulletin* 85/86 no.1 (1994), 40-57.

[34]On how the theme of social justice has been taken further by the post-conciliar Church, see Gustavo Gutiérrez, "The Church and the Poor: A Latin American Perspective," in *Reception*, 171-93. Gutiérrez

have frequently and vigorously underscored the intrinsic unity of the three activities of the Church's mission: inculturation, interreligious dialogue, and liberation.[35]

7. Another significant development in the Asian Churches as the result of Vatican II is the commitment to and work for ecumenical unity. Church division, which was the heritage of historical circumstances in the West and was imported into Asia by denominational missionaries, is perceived as a hindrance to the mission of the Church.[36] Whereas the Protestant Churches had long been engaged in organizing various church unions (e.g., the Tranquebar and Tambaran Conferences), the Catholic

---

describes the reception of Vatican II by the Latin American Church as follows: "... the Latin American Church ... has made its own the insights of John XXIII vis-à-vis the Church of the poor, and it has tried to interpret the great themes of the Council in light of this insight.... There is no question, however, of a simple, mechanical application of Vatican II. Rather, the Latin American Church is endeavoring in a profoundly mature way to be faithful, with the Council, to the Lord of history and to a Church that is beginning to become truly universal, as Karl Rahner has said" (193). The same thing should be said about the Asian Churches.

[35]See James H. Kroeger, *Human Promotion as an Integral Dimension of the Church's Mission of Evangelization: A Philippine Experience and Perspective Since Vatican II—1965-1984* (Rome: Pontificia Università Gregoriana, 1985); Sung-Hae Kim, "Liberation and Inculturation: Two Streams of Doing Theology With Asian Resources," *EAPR* 24/4 (1987), 379-91; Peter C. Phan, "Human Development and Evangelization: The First to the Sixth Plenary Assembly of the Federation of Asian Bishops' Conference," *Studia Missionalia* 47 (1998), 205-27.

[36]For a survey of the ecumenical movement in Asia, see the helpful entry "Ecumenical Movement" in *A Dictionary of Asian Christianity*, ed. Scott Sunquist (Grand Rapids, MI: Eerdmans, 2001), 258-65.

Church took on the work of ecumenical dialogue seriously only after Vatican II.[37] Nevertheless, it must be said that in the Catholic Churches of Asia, ecumenical dialogue has taken the second place, with the primary emphasis given to interreligious dialogue. Happily, in recent years, collaboration between the Federation of Asian Bishops' Conferences (FABC) and the Christian Conference of Asia (CCA) has been taking place. In 1994 the two bodies founded the Asian Movement for Christian Unity (AMCU). So far the movement has had three meetings, the first (1996) with the theme "Theology of Ecumenism"; the second (1998) with the theme "Ecumenical Formation as Churches of Asia Move Towards the Next Millennium"; and the third (2001) with the theme "Giving Shape to a New Ecumenical Vision of Asia."[38]

8. A noteworthy recent development in the Asian Churches is the founding of several missionary societies. This phenomenon can be regarded as a reception of Vatican II's emphasis on mission *ad gentes* as the task of the whole Church, including the so-called mission territories.[39] Currently there are six *ad gentes* missionary societies: Mission Society of the Philippines, Missionary Society of Saint Thomas the Apostle (India), Catholic

---

[37] See Masatoshi Doi, "Vatican II and Ecumenism," *Japan Christian Quarterly* 33 (Summer 1967), 177-81; E. R. Hambye, "All-India Seminar on Ecumenism," *Clergy Monthly* 35 (1971), 84-86; Prudent De Letter, "Ecumenical Developments after the Council," *Clergy Monthly* 31 (1967), 23-29.

[38] See Asian Movement For Christian Unity III, *Giving Shape to a New Ecumenical Vision. FABC Papers,* No. 99 (Hong Kong: FABC, 16 Caine Road, 2001).

[39] See *Ad Gentes Divinitus,* no. 2: "The Church on earth is by its very nature missionary...." See also John Paul II's encyclical *Redemptoris Missio* (1990).

Foreign Mission Society of Korea, Missionary Society of Heralds of Good News (India), Missionary Society of Thailand, and Lorenzo Ruiz Mission Society (Philippines).[40]

9. So far we have discussed the various areas in which the Churches of Asia have responded to the challenges of Vatican II. However important these activities may be, they could not have been successfully carried out without the guidance and encouragement of the Federation of Asian Bishops' Conferences (FABC) whose establishment is certainly a landmark in the history of Christianity in Asia.[41] During the meeting of 180 Asian bishops in Manila in November 1970, on the occasion of the visit of Pope Paul VI, initial steps were taken for the organization of the FABC. These were completed in Hong Kong on 24-25 August 1972, when the statutes of the FABC were accepted, confirmed and submitted to the Holy See for approval. This approval, granted on 16 November of the same year, marked the official establishment of the FABC. In a sense, the FABC

---

[40]For information on these societies, see James Kroeger, *Asia-Church in Mission: Exploring Ad Gentes Mission Initiatives of the Local Churches in Asia in the Vatican II Era* (Quezon City, Philippines: Claretian Publications, 1999).

[41]For a collection of the FABCs and its various Offices' documents, see Gaudencio Rosales and C. G. Arévalo, eds., *For All Peoples of Asia: Federation of Asian Bishops' Conferences. Documents from 1970 to 1991* (Maryknoll, NY: Orbis Books, 1991) and Franz-Josef Eilers, ed., *For All the Peoples of Asia: Federation of Asian Bishops' Conferences. Documents from 1992 to 1996* (Quezon City, Philippines: Claretian Publications, 1997); idem, ed., *For All the Peoples of Asia: Federation of Asian Bishops' Conferences. Documents from 1997 to 2001* (Quezon City, Philippines: Claretian Publications, 2002) [idem, ed., *For All the Peoples of Asia: Federation of Asian Bishops' Conferences. Documents from 2002-2006* (Quezon City, Philippines: Claretian Publications, 2007]. These volumes will be cited as *For All Peoples of Asia*, followed by their respective years of publication.

is both the concrete result of the reception of Vatican II and its effective instrument of implementation.[42]

Structurally, the Federation has no president, only a secretary general, whose task is to execute the policies and decisions of the Federation with the assistance of a central secretariat. The highest body of the Federation is the Plenary Assembly, convened ordinarily once every four years [nine so far (2010)], in which the presidents of each conference and its delegates participate. The direction of the FABC is carried out by the Central Committee made up of the presidents of the member conferences and a standing committee of elected members. To assist the operations of the Federation, there are various offices for various aspects of Christian life. Thus, there are nine such offices, each with several episcopal members: Evangelization, Social Communication, Laity, Human Development, Education and Student Chaplaincy, Ecumenical and Interreligious Affairs, Theological Concerns, Consecrated Life, and Clergy.[43]

There is no doubt that the FABC, through its Plenary Assemblies and Offices, has made an immense contribution to the life of the Asian Churches. Its Third Plenary Assembly offered the following assessment of what the FABC had done for

---

[42]For a brief history and evaluation of the FABC, see Felix Wilfrid, "The Federation of Asian Bishops' Conferences (FABC): Orientations, Challenges and Impact," in *For All Peoples of Asia* (1991), xxiii-xxx. The current [2005] members of the FABC are: 14 episcopal conferences as full members (Bangladesh, China, India, Indonesia, Japan, Korea, Laos-Cambodia, Malaysia-Singapore-Brunei, Myanmar [Burma], Pakistan, the Philippines, Sri Lanka, Thailand, and Vietnam) and 10 associate members (Hong Kong, Kazakhstan, Kyrgyzstan, Macao, Mongolia, Nepal, Siberia, Tajikistan, Turkmenistan, and Uzbekistan).

[43]For an organizational chart of the FABC, see *For All the Peoples of Asia* (1997), 314.

the Asian Churches: creation of the bonds of mutual knowledge and understanding, of friendship and solidarity, involving a sharing of thought, prayer, theological and pastoral orientations, and even of some material and personnel resources; joint study and reflection, leading to a greater community of vision, discernment, decisions, responses to common or similar situations and challenges.[44]

It is to be noted that the grand vision of both Vatican II and the FABC for the Church has not always been enfleshed in concrete actions and programs. This failure was not due to a lack of goodwill, much less to an open opposition to the Council, as it happened in the West, for instance, in the case of Archbishop Marcel Lefebvre and various ultraconservative groups.[45] Rather it is to be attributed to various factors most of which are beyond the control of the Asian Churches, such as hostile governments (e.g., in China and Vietnam) and the lack of resources. As Felix Wilfred has put it correctly, "The resources at the disposal of the bishops in Asia are so limited that they feel helpless in implementing the grand vision of the FABC."[46] And, we may add, of Vatican II as well.[47]

The Asian Synod: The Asian Churches Reaching Maturity. What the Asian bishops did not or could not do at the Second Vatican Council, their successors did splendidly

---

[44] See *For All Peoples of Asia* (1992), 49.

[45] On the opposition to Vatican II, see Daniele Menozzi, "Opposition to the Council (1966-84)" in *Reception*, 325-348.

[46] *For All Peoples of Asia* (1992), xxx.

[47] One of the themes of Vatican II that has not been sufficiently received in Asia is ecumenism. The focus has been more on interreligious dialogue than on ecumenical dialogue.

during the Special Assembly of the Synod of Bishops for Asia, the "Asian Synod" for short. Convened by Pope John Paul II as part of the celebration of the Jubilee Year 2000, the Asian Synod met in Rome, 19 April - 13 May 1998. The theme chosen by the pope for it was "Jesus Christ the Savior and His Mission of Love and Service in Asia: 'That They May Have Life, and Have It Abundantly' (John 10:10)."

In preparation for the synod, the General Secretariat of the Synod of Bishops sent out to all the bishops of Asia an outline of the themes to be discussed called the Lineamenta, and solicited their comments and suggestions.[48] On the basis of these, the Secretariat prepared an Instrumentum laboris presenting the issues to be discussed by the synod. This

---

[48]It is well known that criticisms of the lineamenta were sharp, some of which came from episcopal conferences, in particular the Japanese bishops. For other evaluations, see, for instance, Chrys McVey, "The Asian Synod: What Is at Stake," East Asian Pastoral Review (EAPR) 35/1 (1998), 143-146; Michael Amaladoss, "Expectations from the Synod for Asia," Vidyajyoti: Journal of Theology Reflection (VJTR) 62 (1998), 144-151; G. Gisbert-Sauch, "The Lineamenta for the Asian Synod: Presentation and Comment," VJTR 61 (1997), 8-17; Paul Puthanangady, "Lineamenta for the Asian Synod," Jeevadhara XXVII, 160 (1997), 231-248: Kuncheria Pathil, "Lineamenta for the Asian Synod: Some Observations and Comments," Jeedvadhara XXVII, 160 (1997), 249-259; J. Constantine Manalel, "The Jesus Movement and the Asian Renaissance: Some Random Reflections for the Asian Synod," Jeevadhara XXVII (1997), 133-153; Francisco Claver, "Personal Thoughts on the Asian Synod," EAPR 35, 2 (1998), 241-248; S. Arokiasamy, "Synod for Asia: An Ecclesial Event of Communion and Shared Witness of Faith," VJTR 62/ 9 (1998), 666-675; Gali Bali, "Asian Synod and Concerns of the Local Church," Jeevadhara 27 (1998), 297-330; John Mansford Prior, "A Tale of Two Synods: Observations on the Special Assembly for Asia," VJTR 62 (1998), 654-665; and   Luis Antonio Tagle, "The Synod for Asia as Event," EAPR 35/ 3 & 4 (1998), 366-378.

working document was later summarized in a text called the *Relatio ante disceptationem*. The synod began with 191 eight-minute "interventions" by synod participants. A summary of these interventions, called the *Relatio post disceptationem*, together with a list of questions, was used as the basis for group discussions. At the end of these discussions 59 "propositions," expressing the consensus of the synod participants, were compiled and voted upon. They were then submitted to the Pope for his use in writing the post-synodal Apostolic Exhortation. On 6 November 1999, John Paul II promulgated *Ecclesia in Asia* in New Delhi, India, in which the Pope said he wished "to share with the Church in Asia and throughout the world the fruits of the special assembly."[49]

In terms of theology, the Asian Synod did not introduce anything novel, beyond what has been said by the various Plenary Assemblies and documents of the FABC. What was new is not what the Asian bishops said but *that* they said it and *how* and *where* they said it. In front of the pope and the Roman Curia, with surprising boldness and candor, humbly but forcefully, the Asian bishops affirmed that the Churches of Asia not only learn from but also have something to teach the Church of Rome as well as the universal Church, precisely from their experiences as Churches not simply *in* but *of* Asia. What was being proposed is not a new doctrine but a new way of being Church, namely, being truly *Asian* Churches through the triple dialogue with the Asian poor, Asian cultures, and Asian religions. In the 191 interventions on the floor and in the small group

---

[49]*Ecclesia in Asia*, no. 4. For a collection of the documents of the Asian Synod and the text of *Ecclesia in Asia,* see Peter C. Phan (ed.), *The Asian Synod: Texts and Commentaries* (Maryknoll, NY: Orbis Books, 2002); see also: James H. Kroeger and Peter C. Phan (eds.), *The Future of the Asian Churches: The Asian Synod and Ecclesia in Asia* (Quezon City, Philippines: Claretian Publications, 2002).

discussions, again and again it was affirmed that it is imperative that the Church in Asia be truly Asian, otherwise it will have no future. Appeal was frequently made to Vatican II's ecclesiology, expressed in the Dogmatic Constitution on the Church, that the Church is a *koinonia*, a "communion of communities." Therefore, it was pointed out, the mode of operation in the Church must be characterized by affective and effective collegiality.[50]

Furthermore, this new way of being Church in Asia demands a new ecclesiology. This is a theme repeatedly emphasized by the FABC, especially in its third and fifth Plenary Assemblies in Bangkok in 1982 and in Bandung, Indonesia in 1990 respectively. This ecclesiology, in a sort of Copernican revolution, de-centers the Church in the sense that it makes the center of the Christian life, not the Church, but the reign of God. The mission of Christians in Asia is not to expand the Church and its institutional structures (*plantatio ecclesiae*) in order to enlarge the sphere of influence for the Church over the society, but to be a transparent sign and effective instrument of the saving presence of the reign of God, the reign of justice, peace and love, of which the Church is a seed.

The significance of the Asian Synod lies, then, not so much in what its Asian participants have said as in being the sign that with it the Churches of Asia have reached maturity. They have arrived at this stage because, in appropriating the teaching of Vatican II, they have set out consciously to put into practice what they call the "Asian Integral Pastoral Approach" (AsIPA)

---

[50]It has been noted that among the themes of Vatican II that have been insufficiently received, collegiality stands out. See Lukas Vischer, "The Reception of the Debate on Collegiality," in *Reception*, 233-48.

towards a "New Way of Being Church in Asia."[51] The goal of this approach is to develop "genuine Christian communities in Asia—Asian in their way of thinking, praying, communicating their own Christ-experience to others."[52] Or to put it in terms of Pope John XXIII's vision for Vatican II, quoted above, the task is to achieve "a step forward toward a doctrinal penetration and a formation of consciousness in faithful and perfect conformity to the authentic doctrine," but always in truly and authentically Asian terms.

With the Asian Synod in Rome the Asian Churches have made a full circle. It was from the Second Vatican Council held in Rome that they had learned how to be Church, "receiving" and appropriating the Council's ecclesiology and the various reforms coming out of it. At the Asian Synod, the Asian Churches returned to Rome and showed how well they have "received" Vatican II and as a result had something to teach the Church of Rome and the Church universal. [NOTE: This text was received in late 2005; sincere gratitude is expressed to the author for his contribution. - Editor]

---

[51]See *For All Peoples of Asia* (1997), 107-11 and 137-39.

[52]*For All Peoples of Asia* (1992), 70.

13

BRIEF CHRONICLE OF VATICAN II

James H. Kroeger, M.M.

January 25, 1959: Pope John XXIII at Saint Paul's Outside the Walls announces his intention to summon a Council.

June 5, 1960: Pope John establishes the preparatory commissions.

December 25, 1961: Pope John in the apostolic constitution *Humanae Salutis* convokes the Council.

July 20, 1962: Invitations are sent to separated Christian Churches and Communities to send delegate-observers to the Council.

September 11, 1962: Pope John addresses the world, asking for prayers for the Council.

October 11, 1962: The Second Vatican Ecumenical Council solemnly opens. John XXIII gives his opening address: *Gaudet Mater Ecclesia.*

October 12, 1962: The Council adjourns at its first meeting to prepare to elect its own commission members rather than accept those appearing on the prepared lists.

October 20, 1962: The Council issues its "Message to Humanity."

November 27, 1962: The first of the lay observers (men and women) is invited to the Council.

December 4, 1962: Cardinal Suenens proposes redrafting the schema on the Church, with two emphases, *ad intra* (the nature of the Church) and *ad extra* (the Church's mission in the world); proposal is enthusiastically accepted.

December 8, 1962: The First Session of the Council concludes without any completed results or approved documents.

April 11, 1963: John XXIII issues his encyclical *Pacem in Terris.*

June 3, 1963: Pope John XXIII dies.

June 21, 1963: Pope Paul VI is elected and announces his intention to continue the Council.

September 29, 1963: The Second Session of the Council opens.

December 4, 1963: The Second Session of the Council closes with the promulgation of the Constitution on the Sacred Liturgy and the Decree on Social Communication.

January 4-6, 1964: Pope Paul makes an ecumenical journey to the Holy Land and meets with Patriarch Athenagoras.

May 19, 1964: Pope Paul creates the Secretariat for Non-Christian Religions [renamed Pontifical Council for Interreligious Dialogue in 1988].

September 14, 1964: The Third Session of the Council opens.

November 14-21, 1964:   The so-called "Black Week" unfolds, revealing tensions on issues such as religious liberty, relations with non-Christians, and the role of the Church in the modern world.

November 21, 1964:   The Third Session closes with the promulgation of the Dogmatic Constitution on the Church, the Decree on Ecumenism, and the Decree on Eastern Catholic Churches.   Pope Paul proclaims the title of Mary as Mother of the Church.

December 2-5, 1964:   Paul VI travels to India for Eucharistic Congress.

March 7, 1965:   The reformed Eucharistic liturgy is inaugurated; Pope Paul celebrates Mass in the vernacular.

September 14, 1965:   The fourth and final session of the Council opens.

September 15, 1965:   Pope Paul in the apostolic constitution *Apostolica Sollicitudo* issues the norms governing the new Episcopal Synod [Synod of Bishops] established to assist him in governing the Church.

October 4-5, 1965:   Pope Paul travels to New York to address the United Nations General Assembly; he reports to the Council about his visit.

October 28, 1965:   The following documents are promulgated: Decree on the Bishops' Pastoral Office in the Church; Decree on the Renewal of Religious Life; Decree on Priestly Formation; Declaration on Christian Education; Declaration on the Relationship of the Church to Non-Christian Religions.

November 18, 1965: The Dogmatic Constitution on Divine Revelation and the Decree on the Apostolate of the Laity are promulgated. Pope Paul announces the beginning of the reform of the Roman Curia, the introduction of the beatification process of Popes Pius XII and John XXIII, a Jubilee period, and the convocation of the Synod of Bishops not later than 1967.

December 4, 1965: At Saint Paul Outside the Walls, where John XXIII first announced the Council, an ecumenical prayer service is held with the purpose of promoting Christian unity.

December 6, 1965: Pope Paul issues a *motu proprio* inaugurating the reform of the Roman Curia.

December 7, 1965: The following documents are promulgated: Declaration on Religious Freedom; Decree on the Ministry and Life of Priests; Decree on the Church's Missionary Activity; and, Pastoral Constitution on the Church in the Modern World. At Istanbul and Vatican City, a joint declaration lifts the mutual excommunications between Greeks and Latins (1054).

December 8, 1965: The Second Vatican Ecumenical Council solemnly closes in Saint Peter's Square. The messages addressed to various sectors of society are read.

November 28-December 8, 1985: An extraordinary synod of bishops is held on the twentieth anniversary of the close of Vatican II to study and promote the fruits of the Council.

September 3, 2000: Pope John XXIII, "Pope of Vatican II," is beatified.

May 1, 2011: Pope John Paul II, a participant in Vatican II, is beatified.

NOTE: This brief chronicle of the Council is drawn from the works of the following authors: W. Abbott, G. Alberigo, J. Gallagher, B. Huebsch, and J. O'Malley.

14

POPULAR BIBLIOGRAPHY OF VATICAN II

James H. Kroeger, M.M.

I. ORIGINAL DOCUMENTS

Abbott, W. and **J. Gallagher** (eds). *The Documents of Vatican II.* New York: America Press, Guild Press, and Association Press, 1966.

Flannery, A. (ed). *Vatican Council II: The Basic Sixteen Documents* (Inclusive Language Translation). Northport, NY: Costello Publishing Company and Dublin, Ireland: Dominican Publications, 1996.

NOTE: Complete texts of the Vatican II documents are available on line in several locations; two are provided here:

(A) EWTN: www.ewtn.com/expert/answers/
vatican_ii_docs.htm
(B) Vatican: www.vatican.va/archive/hist_
councils/ii_vatican_council/index.htm

II. SUMMARIES

Hahnenberg, E. *A Concise Guide to the Documents of Vatican II.* Cincinnati: St. Anthony Messenger Press, 2007.

Heffernan, V. (ed). *Outlines of the 16 Documents: Vatican II.* New York: The America Press, 1966.

III. DICTIONARY AND ENCYCLOPEDIA ENTRIES

Dictionary of Fundamental Theology [Latourelle-Fisichella]. "Vatican II" [Latourelle: 1151-1162]. New York: Crossroad, 1994.

New Catholic Encyclopedia: Second Edition: XIV [Marthaler *et al.*]. "Vatican Council II" [Komonchak-Trisco: 407-418]. New York: Thomson-Gale, 2003.

The New Dictionary of Theology [Komonchak *et al.*]. "Vatican Council II" [Komonchak: 1072-1077]. Wilmington: Michael Glazier, 1987.

IV. MULTI-VOLUME COMMENTARIES

Anderson, F. (ed). *Council Daybook: Vatican II* (3 volumes). Washington: National Catholic Welfare Conference, 1965-1966.

Hastings, A. *A Concise Guide to the Documents of the Second Vatican Council* (2 volumes). London: Darton, Longman and Todd, 1968.

Huebsch, B. *Vatican II in Plain English* (3 volumes). Allen, TX: Thomas More, 1997.

Latourelle, R. (ed). *Vatican II: Assessment and Perspectives* (3 volumes). New York: Paulist Press, 1988-1989.

V. BOOKS

Alberigo, G. *A Brief History of Vatican II.* Maryknoll, NY: Orbis Books, 2006.

Coyle, K. (ed). *Forty Years of Vatican II and the Churches of Asia and the Pacific: Looking Back and Moving Forward.* Manila: East Asian Pastoral Institute, 2005.

Doyle, D. *The Church Emerging from Vatican II.* Mystic, CT: Twenty-third Publications, 1992.

Fesquet, H. *The Drama of Vatican II.* New York: Random House, 1967.

Kloppenburg, B. *The Ecclesiology of Vatican II.* Chicago: Franciscan Herald Press, 1974.

Kroeger, J. *The Second Vatican Council and the Church in Asia: Readings and Reflections.* Hong Kong: FABC, 2006.

Madges, W. (ed). *Vatican II: Forty Years Later.* Maryknoll, NY: Orbis Books, 2006.

O'Collins, G. *Living Vatican II: The 21st Council for the 21st Century.* New York: Paulist Press, 2006.

O'Malley, J. *What Happened at Vatican II.* Cambridge, MA: Harvard University Press, 2008.

Pennington, B. *Vatican II: We've Only Just Begun.* New York: Crossroad, 1994.

Ratzinger, J. (Benedict XVI). *Theological Highlights of Vatican II.* New York: Paulist Press, 1966 and 2009.

Rynne, X. *Vatican Council II.* Maryknoll, NY: Orbis Books, 1999.

Suenens, L.J. *A New Pentecost?* London: Darton, Longman & Todd, 1975.

Sullivan, M. *101 Questions and Answers on Vatican II.* New York: Paulist Press, 2002.

Von Galli, M. and **B. Moosbrugger.** *The Council and the Future.* New York: McGraw-Hill Book Company, 1966 [Excellent original photographs].

Wiltgen, R. *The Rhine Flows into the Tiber: A History of Vatican II.* New York: Hawthorne Books, 1967.

VI. ARTICLES

Capovilla, L. "Pope John and His Council," *The Tablet* 246:7944 (November 7, 1992): 1388-1391.

Cummings, O. Six-part series on the "Popes of Vatican II" in *Emmanuel* 115-116 (2009-2010): "John XXIII" [232-239, 244-250]; "Paul VI" [34-47, 52-56]; "John Paul I" [329-333]; "John Paul II" [388-410]; "Benedict XVI" Part I [517-527, 530-534], Part II [36-47, 51-53].

Dulles, A. [A] "Vatican II Reform: The Basic Principles," *Church* 1:2 (Summer, 1985): 3-10. [B] "Vatican II and the Church's Purpose," *Theology Digest* 32:4 (1985): 341-352.

Hereford, A. "Consecrated Life in the Ecclesiology of Vatican II," *Review for Religious* 70:2 (2011): 194-200.

Hurley, D. "The Struggle of Vatican II," *Church* 17:1 (2001): 17-24.

Ker, I. "The Life of John Henry Newman: The Father of Vatican II," *L'Osservatore Romano* 42:29 (July 22, 2009): 7.

Komonchak, J. **[A]** "Ecclesiology of Vatican II," *Origins* 28:44 (April 22, 1999): 763-768. **[B]** "Vatican II as an 'Event'," *Theology Digest* 46:4 (1999): 337-352. **[C]** "Remembering Good Pope John, *Commonweal* 127:14 (August 11, 2000): 11-16. **[D]** "The Ongoing Challenge: Forty Years after Vatican II," *Ligourian* 90:8 (2002): 11-14. **[E]** "Novelty in Continuity: Pope Benedict's Interpretation of Vatican II," *America* 200:3 (February 2, 2009): 10-14, 16.

Kroeger, J. "Philippine Participation in the Second Vatican Ecumenical Council," *Philippiniana Sacra* 42:124 (2007): 173-182.

National Catholic Reporter. Special Issue: "Vatican II, Forty Years Later: The Council that Keeps Changing the Church," 38:42 (October 4, 2002): 36 pages.

O'Malley, J. "What Happened and Did Not Happen at Vatican II," *Theology Digest* 53:4 (Winter 2006): 331-344.

Pecklers, K. "Vatican II and the Liturgical Renewal: An Unfinished Agenda," *East Asian Pastoral Review* 42:1-2 (2005): 26-44.

Rahner, K. **[A]** "The Lasting Significance of Vatican II," *Theology Digest* 28:3 (1980): 221-225. **[B]** "Basic Theological Interpretation of the Second Vatican Council" 77-89 in: *Concern for the Church: Theological Investigations 20.* New York: Crossroad, 1981.

Ratzinger, J. (Benedict XVI). **[A]** "The Ecclesiology of Vatican II," *Origins* 15 (1985): 370-376. **[B]** "Interpreting Vatican II," *Origins* 35:32 (January 26, 2006): 534-539.

The Tablet. [A] "The Vatican II Revolution" [series of fifteen articles on the twentieth anniversary of Vatican II] 236-237 (October 1982-February 1983). [B] "How Vatican II Changed the Church" [series of eleven articles on the fortieth anniversary of Vatican II] 256 (October-December, 2002).

VII. VIDEO AND MEDIA RESOURCES (random listing)

Vatican II: The Faithful Revolution. (Thomas More: 300 min.). This series of five one-hour presentations includes: **I.** *Genius of the Heart,* **II.** *Inspired Awakening,* **III.** *Human Dignity,* **IV.** *A World Transformed,* **V.** *The Dynamics of Hope.*

Third Millennium: Vatican II: "A Civilization of Love." (Hallel Communications: 270 min.). This series of nine thirty-minute presentations includes: **I.** *Vatican II in History,* **II.** *Liturgy,* **III.** *Laity,* **IV.** *Evangelization,* **V.** *Ecumenism,* **VI.** *Religious Freedom,* **VII.** *The Word,* **VIII.** *Mary,* **IX.** *After the Council.*

Concilium Vaticanum II. (Vatican Television Center: 60 min.).

Author of Reform: The Cardinal Suenens Story. (Journey Films: 60 min.).

John XXIII: The Pope of Peace. (Ignatius Press: 200 min.).

Paul VI: The Pope in the Tempest. (Ignatius Press: 200 min.).

Bernardin: The Life and Legacy of Cardinal Joseph Bernadin. (Journey / Frost Productions: 60 min.).

VIII. INTERNET SOURCES (random listing)

vatican.va/archive/hist.... This site contains the complete documents of Vatican II in several Western, Asian, and African languages.

stjosef.at/council/search   This site provides a fulltext search of all Vatican Council II documents.

NOTE: For an extensive bibliography, consult *Documents of Vatican Council II,* edited by J. Kroeger and published in 2011 by Paulines (Daughters of Saint Paul) in Pasay City, Philippines.

BOOKS BY JAMES H. KROEGER *

DOCUMENTS OF VATICAN COUNCIL II.
Pasay City, Philippines: Paulines, 2011.

A FIERY FLAME: ENCOUNTERING GOD'S WORD.
Quezon City, Philippines: Claretian Publications,
Insta Publications, and Jesuit Communications, 2010.

JESUS: A PORTRAIT (Philippine Edition)
Quezon City, Philippines: Claretian Publications
and Jesuit Communications, 2010.

MIGRATION: OPENING PATHWAYS OF THE CHURCH'S MISSION.
Quezon City, Philippines: Scalabrini Migration Center, 2010.

DIALOGUE: INTERPRETIVE KEY FOR THE LIFE OF THE CHURCH IN ASIA.
Hong Kong: Federation of Asian Bishops' Conferences, 2010.

THEOLOGY FROM THE HEART OF ASIA: I - II.
Quezon City, Philippines: Claretian Publications, 2008.

**ARE NOT OUR HEARTS BURNING? 75 YEARS OF THE PONTIFICAL
MISSION SOCIETIES OF THE PHILIPPINES.**
Sampaloc, Manila: Pontifical Mission Societies, 2008.

* This list includes books produced by James Kroeger as author/editor,
either alone or in collaboration with others.

FABC PAPERS PERIODIC INDEX: Papers 101-125 (2001-2008).
Hong Kong: Federation of Asian Bishops' Conferences, 2008.

THE SECOND VATICAN COUNCIL AND THE CHURCH IN ASIA:
READINGS AND REFLECTIONS.
Hong Kong: Federation of Asian Bishops' Conferences, 2006.

ONCE UPON A TIME IN ASIA: STORIES OF HARMONY AND PEACE.
North American Edition: Maryknoll, New York: Orbis Books, 2006.
Asian Edition: Quezon City, Philippines: Claretian Publications and
    Jesuit Communications, 2006.
Polish Edition: Pewnego Razu w Azji. Kraków: Wydawnictwo WAM, 2007.
Vietnamese Edition: Vietnamese Institute of Philosophy & Religion, 2008.
Thai Edition: Bangkok: Catholic Social Communications of Thailand, 2008.
Italian Edition: Armonie: Volti dell'Asia, Volti di Dio. Bologna: EMI, 2008.
Chinese-English Bilingual Edition: Taipei: Kuangchi Cultural Group, 2008.
Bahasa-Indonesia Edition: Kisah-kisah Harmoni dan Damai.
    Yogyakarta, Indonesia: Penerbit Kanisius, 2008.
Bengali Edition: Dhaka, Bangladesh: Holy Spirit Major Seminary, 2010.

INCULTURATION IN ASIA: DIRECTIONS, INITIATIVES, AND OPTIONS.
Hong Kong: Federation of Asian Bishops' Conferences, 2005.

THE CHALLENGE OF RELIGIOUS DIVERSITY IN MIGRATION.
Quezon City, Philippines: Scalabrini Migration Center, 2005.

BECOMING LOCAL CHURCH:
HISTORICAL, THEOLOGICAL AND MISSIOLOGICAL ESSAYS.
Quezon City, Philippines: Claretian Publications, 2003.

LOCAL CHURCH, DIALOGUE AND CONVERSION.
Hong Kong: Federation of Asian Bishops' Conferences, 2003.

SUGINLI ANG KALIBUTAN: CEBUANO TRANSLATION OF: TELL THE
WORLD: CATECHETICAL MODULES FOR MISSION ANIMATION.
Cebu City, Philippines: Archdiocesan Commission on Mission, 2003.

THE FUTURE OF THE ASIAN CHURCHES:
THE ASIAN SYNOD AND *ECCLESIA IN ASIA.*
Quezon City, Philippines: Claretian Publications, 2002.

SONS OF SAN JOSE: THE JOSEFINO SPIRIT—A PROFILE.
Quezon City, Philippines: San Jose Seminary Alumni Association, 2002.

TELLING GOD'S STORY: NATIONAL MISSION CONGRESS 2000.
Quezon City, Philippines: Claretian Publications, 2001.

FABC PAPERS COMPREHENSIVE INDEX: 1976-2001.
Hong Kong: Federation of Asian Bishops' Conferences, 2001.

TELL THE WORLD: CATECHETICAL MODULES FOR MISSION ANIMATION.
Quezon City, Philippines: Claretian Publications, 2000.

ECCLESIA IN ASIA: COMMENTARIES.
Shillong, India: Mission Today Editions, 2000.

MISSION ANIMATION RESOURCE KIT (MARK).
Manila, Philippines: Catholic Bishops' Conference of the Philippines, 2000.

ASIA-CHURCH IN MISSION.
Quezon City, Philippines: Claretian Publications, 1999.

LIVING MISSION IN ASIA.
Hong Kong: Federation of Asian Bishops' Conferences, 1999.

REMEMBERING OUR BISHOP JOSEPH W. REGAN, M.M.
Quezon City, Philippines: Claretian Publications, 1998.

CONTEMPORARY MISSION ISSUES.
A Series of eleven pamphlets on Mission Issues.
Maryknoll, New York: Maryknoll Press, 1995-1997.

LIVING MISSION: CHALLENGES IN EVANGELIZATION TODAY.
North American Edition: Maryknoll, New York: Orbis Books, 1994, 2009.
Asian Edition: Quezon City, Philippines: Claretian Publications, 1994.

MISSION TODAY: CONTEMPORARY THEMES IN MISSIOLOGY.
Hong Kong: Federation of Asian Bishops' Conferences, 1991.

INTERRELIGIOUS DIALOGUE: CATHOLIC PERSPECTIVES.
Davao City, Philippines: Mission Studies Institute, 1990.

KNOWING CHRIST JESUS: A CHRISTOLOGICAL SOURCEBOOK.
Quezon City, Philippines: Claretian Publications, 1989.

CHURCH TRULY ALIVE: JOURNEY TO THE FILIPINO REVOLUTION.
Davao City, Philippines: Mission Studies Institute, 1988.

ADVANCED CEBUANO COLLOQUIAL EXPRESSIONS.
Davao City, Philippines: Institute of Language and Culture, 1986.

THE PHILIPPINE CHURCH AND EVANGELIZATION: 1965-1984.
Rome, Italy: Gregorian University Press, 1985.